DATE DUE	

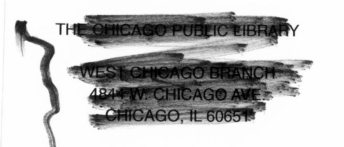

Diseases and Disorders

Chronic Fatigue Syndrome

Titles in the Diseases and Disorders series include:

Diseases and Disorders

Chronic Fatigue Syndrome

by Liesa Abrams

LUCENT
BOOKS®

THOMSON
—————✦————— ™
GALE

San Diego • Detroit • New York • San Francisco • Cleveland
New Haven, Conn. • Waterville, Maine • London • Munich

THOMSON

———————✦——————— ™

GALE

LIBRARY OF CONGRESS CATALOGING-IN-PUBLICATION DATA

Abrams, Liesa.
    Chronic fatigue syndrome / by Liesa Abrams.
      p. cm. — (Diseases and disorders series)
Summary: Examines the symptoms, treatment options, and mystery of chronic fatigue syndrome, ongoing research into its causes, and how to live with this disease.
Includes bibliographical references (p.   ) and index.
    ISBN 1-59018-039-9
   1. Chronic fatigue syndrome—Juvenile literature. [1. Chronic fatigue syndrome. 2. Diseases.] I. Title. II. Series.
    RB150 .F37A275 2003
    616' .0478—dc21

                                           2002009459

Table of Contents

"The Most Difficult Puzzles Ever Devised"

CHARLES BEST, ONE of the pioneers in the search for a cure for diabetes, once explained what it is about medical research that intrigued him so. "It's not just the gratification of knowing one is helping people," he confided, "although that probably is a more heroic and selfless motivation. Those feelings may enter in, but truly, what I find best is the feeling of going toe to toe with nature, of trying to solve the most difficult puzzles ever devised. The answers are there somewhere, those keys that will solve the puzzle and make the patient well. But how will those keys be found?"

Since the dawn of civilization, nothing has so puzzled people—and often frightened them, as well—as the onset of illness in a body or mind that had seemed healthy before. A seizure, the inability of a heart to pump, the sudden deterioration of muscle tone in a small child—being unable to reverse such conditions or even to understand why they occur was unspeakably frustrating to healers. Even before there were names for such conditions, even before they were understood at all, each was a reminder of how complex the human body was, and how vulnerable.

While our grappling with understanding diseases has been frustrating at times, it has also provided some of humankind's most heroic accomplishments. Alexander Fleming's accidental discovery in 1928 of a mold that could be turned into penicillin has resulted in the saving of untold millions of lives. The isolation of the enzyme insulin has reversed what was once a death sentence for anyone with diabetes. There have been great strides in combating conditions for which there is not yet a cure, too. Medicines can help AIDS patients live longer, diagnostic tools such as mammography and ultrasounds can help doctors find tumors while they are treatable, and laser surgery techniques have made the most intricate, minute operations routine.

This "toe-to-toe" competition with diseases and disorders is even more remarkable when seen in a historical continuum. An astonishing amount of progress has been made in a very short time. Just two hundred years ago, the existence of germs as a cause of some diseases was unknown. In fact, it was less than 150 years ago that a British surgeon named Joseph Lister had difficulty persuading his fellow doctors that washing their hands before delivering a baby might increase the chances of a healthy delivery (especially if they had just attended to a diseased patient)!

Each book in Lucent's *Diseases and Disorders* series explores a disease or disorder and the knowledge that has been accumulated (or discarded) by doctors through the years. Each book also examines the tools used for pinpointing a diagnosis, as well as the various means that are used to treat or cure a disease. Finally, new ideas are presented—techniques or medicines that may be on the horizon.

Frustration and disappointment are still part of medicine, for not every disease or condition can be cured or prevented. But the limitations of knowledge are being pushed outward constantly; the "most difficult puzzles ever devised" are finding challengers every day.

Chronic Fatigue Syndrome—More than Just Being Tired

DOCTORS ACROSS THE United States whose patients complain of being constantly tired are increasingly faced with the question of whether they think the problem is chronic fatigue syndrome (CFS). Usually, however, doctors explain that, in fact, CFS is actually an illness that involves far more than just the feeling of being tired.

Despite the growing number of physicians who consider CFS a disease, controversy over the illness continues inside the medical community. Some doctors still question whether CFS even exists, and debate rages among those who do believe in its existence as to whether it is a physical or psychological problem. The intense conflict over these issues has created a good deal of confusion in the public. And much of this confusion begins with the name of the disease itself—chronic *fatigue* syndrome.

Overwhelming, utterly incapacitating fatigue is in fact among the first symptoms a CFS patient experiences. However, this fatigue is only one aspect of the disease. Individuals suffering from CFS—as opposed to simple, if extreme, tiredness—tell remarkably similar stories: Someone who has always been healthy, energetic, and active one day wakes up with something that feels like the flu. The patient has a sore throat, swollen glands, a

headache, a low-grade fever, and is too exhausted to even get out of bed. But then weeks pass and these symptoms do not subside. Meanwhile, any attempt at exercise just makes the patient *more* tired rather than replenishing his or her energy the way exercise would for a normal, healthy person. The patient develops dizziness and balance problems, and no amount of sleep makes the

A chronic fatigue syndrome patient sleeps in her bed. Overwhelming fatigue is one of the first symptoms of CFS.

victim feel refreshed. The patient's stomach becomes upset easily and often, and he or she experiences frequent and sometimes painful urination. Soon, short-term memory starts to falter. The patient is unable to concentrate long enough to read one page of a book, and he or she mixes up words for common household objects. After months have gone by, none of the various symptoms have lessened, while new ones seem to develop every week.

Those who deal with the illness say that it is hard to overstate just how debilitating the symptoms of CFS can be. At a congressional briefing in 1995, infectious disease specialist Dr. Mark Loveless testified that "a CFS patient feels every day effectively the same as an AIDS patient feels two months before death."[1] Many CFS patients are homebound and even bed bound, and report that the simple act of brushing their teeth is utterly exhausting, using up a day's worth of energy. Patients remain helpless while they watch system after system seemingly fail in their bodies, even losing their ability to think clearly.

Because the illness produces so many symptoms beyond fatigue—many of them incapacitating—a large percentage of both the doctors who treat the disease and their patients have protested the naming of the disease "chronic fatigue syndrome." They argue that this name does not accurately represent the breadth of symptoms and also has contributed to the failure of many doctors and policy makers to take the disease seriously. As one strong opponent to calling the illness "chronic fatigue syndrome" argues:

> The euphemistic, benign-sounding name [suggests] a trivial, volitional disability, one that could be shrugged off with vitamins, aerobic exercise, stress reduction, a good night's sleep, or sheer willpower. . . . More profoundly, the name [camouflages] the nature of the illness itself: the fatigue in "chronic fatigue syndrome" [is] merely a symptom and, compared to the neurologic dysfunction . . . a sometimes unimportant one at that. . . . If diseases were named after symptoms, leukemia too might well be called "chronic fatigue syndrome" and diabetes "chronic thirst syndrome."[2]

An alternative name, one used by various health professionals and authors on the topic, is chronic fatigue immune dysfunction syndrome (CFIDS), which many experts feel better describes the nature of the disease. People whose lives have been seriously impacted by the illness hope that with a different name, their disease can be given more attention and thus be better understood.

The failure of some doctors and government officials to take CFS seriously is frustrating to those who suffer from or treat the illness. Also frustrating is the failure so far of researchers to identify its cause. While there are many theories on a cause, and there is evidence to *support* some of these theories, there is still no definitive proof as to what causes CFS, which is why a minority of the medical community still questions if CFS is truly a disease with an organic origin.

CFS patients often find themselves homebound and sometimes too exhausted even to get out of bed.

Despite the controversy, what is known is that the number of people afflicted with CFS is on the rise. The prevalence of CFS in the United States alone is estimated by some observers to be somewhere around one million, with many calling this estimate conservative. Such numbers have caught the attention of federal policy makers. Since 1995, CFS has been on the Centers for Disease Control and Prevention's list of "Priority 1 New and Reemerging Infectious Diseases," meaning that CFS is acknowledged as a genuine threat deserving of research dollars.

Unfortunately, even with these developments, CFS remains a mystery. The diagnostic process is complex and challenging, and without a known cure, doctors and alternative health practitioners struggle to find treatment options for the array of symptoms that affect someone with CFS. Many experts are convinced, however, that clues to the puzzle of CFS can be found in a careful examination of its history.

Chapter 1

A Mystery Disease

IN 1869, AMERICAN neurologist Dr. George M. Beard identified a mysterious condition in his patients that had no clear cause, but which left its victims suffering from chronic, extreme fatigue along with a host of other symptoms, including headaches and generalized pain. Beard was unable to find an organic—that is, physical—cause of the condition, so he concluded that it was a psychological disorder causing physical symptoms. In particular, Beard felt the disease had to do with overly aggravated nerves, so he named it "neurasthenia."

Beard continued to study and write about this disease throughout his career, publishing a book on it in 1881 entitled *American Nervousness: Its Causes and Consequences*. In it, Beard mused on what he considered to be the cause of neurasthenia, which he believed was a new disease, one that was somehow related to the complications of life in the late nineteenth century: "The modern differ from the ancient civilizations mainly in these five elements—steam power, the periodical press [newpapers], the telegraph, the sciences, and the mental activity of women. When civilization, plus these five factors, invades any nation, it must carry nervousness and nervous diseases along with it."[3] To support his argument, Beard pointed out that the vast majority of people being diagnosed with neurasthenia belonged to the higher, more educated classes—people who were expected to use their minds more in their daily lives. Beard's treatment for his patients included bed rest—either at home or in a hospital if necessary—nourishing food, and emotional support from family and employers.

Over the years, attention to neurasthenia waned for various reasons. Certainly, as the twentieth century progressed, for instance, the notion that "the mental activity of women" could be so unnatural as to lead to illness came to be seen as unlikely. And while a diagnosis of neurasthenia was somewhat a status symbol in Beard's time, since it identified the patient as a member of a higher social class, neurasthenia eventually became thought of more as another form of simple hysteria, a condition that carried with it a much stronger stigma. Primarily, however, the lack of any proven organic cause kept physicians from concentrating much attention on neurasthenia. Moreover, since psychiatry was becoming accepted as a legitimate field of medicine, a whole new group of professionals was considered available to focus on what was viewed as a psychological problem.

Many experts believe that Dr. George M. Beard was the first doctor to describe the illness now called chronic fatigue syndrome.

Today, however, many experts believe that Beard was the first doctor to identify a physical illness that is now called chronic fatigue syndrome, although they would disagree with Beard's ideas regarding the causes of the disease. These experts also speculate that Beard actually identified an illness that has been around for centuries, pointing to earlier references to diseases, such as muscular rheumatism in the 1680s, that had similar symptoms. Experts also believe that in the years following Beard's initial discovery, many names were given to conditions that were all in fact the same thing: chronic fatigue syndrome.

Outbreaks

While much controversy remains over when CFS first appeared, most researchers now agree that the disease—in some form—can at least be traced back to the 1930s, starting with an outbreak in a Los Angeles hospital in 1934, in which 198 health care workers became ill. Since these individuals displayed symptoms directly following an epidemic of the disease poliomyelitis, they were initially diagnosed with polio. However, this diagnosis was proved incorrect when the patients did not develop paralysis, and none died, a common outcome for polio victims at that time. Also, closer study revealed that the patients had symptoms that polio sufferers did not have. For example, these patients experienced chronic fatigue that was worsened by physical exertion; they also had headaches, intestinal problems, impaired memory, and extreme muscle weakness, among a variety of other symptoms. Mystified, investigators named the disease "neuromyasthenia," without reaching a consensus as to what was causing the symptoms in the infected individuals.

Over the years, other similarly confounding outbreaks occurred throughout the United States and in certain European countries, though slight differences in symptoms kept anyone from being able to forge a definitive link between outbreaks. In 1948, for example, over one thousand people in Iceland became ill with what was labeled "Iceland Disease." Again, the theory was put forward that this was some form of polio. And again, patients did not become paralyzed or die. Outbreaks followed in Austria in 1949, New York State in 1950, England in 1953, and Washington, D.C., in 1953.

The outbreak that gained major attention, however, occurred at the Royal Free Hospital in London in 1955. First, one physician and one nurse were admitted to the hospital with similar symptoms: fatigue, malaise, headaches, and sore throats. Other reported symptoms included muscle weakness, abdominal pain, diarrhea, dizziness, and bladder problems. Over the next few weeks, increasing numbers of hospital personnel developed symptoms, until eventually 292 staff members in total were ill. The hospital had to be shut down for four months. While various

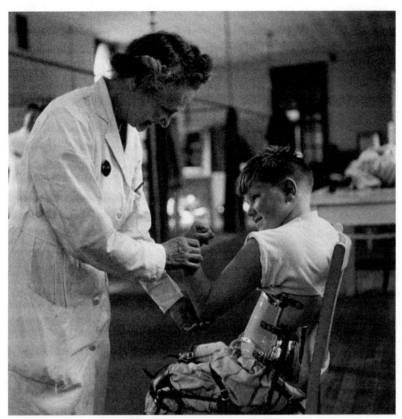

A young polio patient flexes his muscle for his doctor in 1947. Some early outbreaks of CFS were initially thought to be polio.

minor abnormalities were detected with full medical examinations, investigators were still unable to find a specific cause. And strangely, while the disease *did* seem to be spreading (since all of these people who contracted it worked together in one place), only twelve of the hospital's patients became sick with the bizarre symptoms. This is inconsistent with a typical infectious disease outbreak, in which a large number of all people in the location become sick, regardless of what role they play in that location.

The outbreak was so puzzling that researchers who later examined the patients' records concluded that there actually had not been an organic disease at work, but instead the symptoms were attributable to some kind of mass hysteria among the hospital workers. Years later, doctors looked back on the Royal Free disease as the origin of the modern debate as to whether CFS is an organic disease, caused by physical and biological factors, or a psychosomatic one with psychological causes such as anxiety or depression.

Yuppie Victims

The question of whether the illness that would one day be called CFS was organic or psychosomatic was brought back into the spotlight in 1985 when people living in the small resort town of Incline Village near Lake Tahoe, Nevada, became sick. There, perfectly healthy individuals were suddenly bedridden with severe fatigue and other symptoms resembling a serious case of influenza. But the victims failed to improve; after months had passed, they remained just as sick as ever. And others grew ill as well, until nearly two hundred people were afflicted. Drs. Daniel Peterson and Paul Cheney, the local physicians in Incline Village, grew frustrated at their inability to make a diagnosis. Although the patients were feeling severely debilitated by their symptoms, Peterson and Cheney had difficulty finding any serious abnormalities common to all patients, as would be expected if a single contagious disease was at work. In fact, most of the patients' lab results initially appeared the same as they would for a normal, healthy person.

Finally, Peterson and Cheney stumbled on what they believed was a major clue: A large majority of their patients had elevated levels of a virus called the Epstein-Barr virus in their blood. The doctors knew that this virus could cause mononucleosis, a disease characterized by many of the symptoms they saw in their patients. But mononucleosis is not typically as debilitating as the disease with which they were dealing, and it is also only rarely chronic. Peterson and Cheney began to wonder if they were facing an outbreak of a new infectious disease that was somehow connected to the Epstein-Barr virus.

The doctors contacted the Centers for Disease Control and Prevention (CDC), an agency of the federal government that is

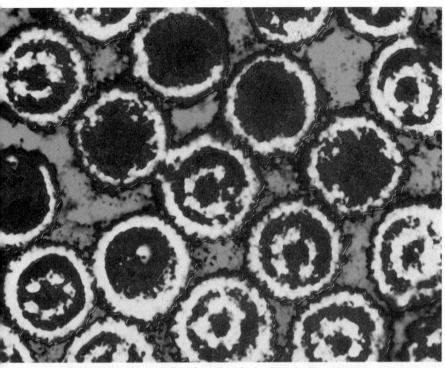

A micrograph shows cells infected with the Epstein-Barr virus.

responsible for identifying and classifying infectious diseases. In response, the CDC sent two of its epidemiologists (doctors who specialize in uncovering causes and connections of diseases) to Lake Tahoe in September 1985. In the end, however, the CDC reported that there was not enough evidence to prove that the Epstein-Barr virus was behind the illness that was affecting so many members of the Incline Village community.

Peterson and Cheney, while aware that the evidence was not supporting their theory, were still disappointed that after this one visit the CDC had closed its investigation. In fact, not only did it discount the Epstein-Barr theory, but the CDC implied that the disease was psychosomatic, since no organic cause could be found.

Lending credence to the notion that the disease was psychosomatic was the fact that so many of the victims were young, upwardly mobile professionals (nicknamed "yuppies" by the mass media), a social class supposedly prone to self-absorption and self-indulgence. Even some who suffered from CFS found the socioeconomic similarities among victims striking. As Hillary Johnson, a journalist and CFS patient herself, put it in a 1987 article for *Rolling Stone* magazine: "So far, most [of the disease's] victims have been between twenty-five and forty-five, with the majority in their thirties. . . . [T]he disease appears to attack only successful, educated professionals while sparing blue-collar workers and the poor. That a disease could mark not only a generation but a class is remarkable."[4]

Despite the pervasive idea that this illness was reserved for a certain group of people, many believed that its reach would expand. Johnson herself went on to predict in her *Rolling Stone* article that the supposition that only a certain demographic group was at risk for the disease would soon be proven wrong.

A young woman suffers from a severe headache caused by CFS.

A Breakthrough Is Made

In fact, an outbreak that proved Johnson's point had already occurred. Dr. David S. Bell, a pediatrician in Lyndonville, New York, in 1985, began seeing patients with a puzzling set of symptoms. The children complained of fatigue, sore throats, stomach pain, and swollen and tender lymph nodes. They appeared to have the flu, but it became clear that it was something more when time passed and the children failed to improve. Meanwhile, more children—and soon adults—began to experience the same symptoms. Bell attempted to get the state health department to show some interest, but he received no assistance from that agency. So he continued his own efforts to pinpoint a cause and arrive at a diagnosis.

Bell recalls having noticed a piece in the newspaper about the epidemic in Lake Tahoe. But while the Lake Tahoe patients' symptoms shared similarities with his patients' symptoms, Bell quickly dismissed the possibility of a connection between the epidemics when he read that the Lake Tahoe epidemic was called "Yuppie Flu" and that it was believed to be a form of hypochondria. He also glimpsed something about two doctors from the area talking about the role of the Epstein-Barr virus. "I knew that whatever we were studying had nothing to do with Yuppies,"[5] Bell later told *Newsweek* magazine. After all, most of his patients were children. Also, a good number tested negative for the Epstein-Barr virus, so there was no obvious connection there either.

Bell was seeing more patients with similar symptoms more regularly and was coming no closer to a diagnosis. By 1987, more than two hundred people in Lyndonville were ill, and Bell had no diagnosis for any of them. But reports started to come in of other patients experiencing similar symptoms in various areas of the country, and the picture finally became clearer when one patient from California explained to Bell that she had previously been told her illness was something called "chronic Epstein-Barr virus syndrome." (This name was being used by doctors even after the Epstein-Barr theory was discounted, since the symptoms of the disease resembled a chronic mononucleosis.) Bell recalled the article about Lake Tahoe, the mention of Epstein-Barr, and made the connection: He was dealing with the same disease that Peterson and Cheney were seeing.

Bell quickly joined forces with Peterson and Cheney, and together they—along with other doctors who were beginning to become aware of and concerned about this new disease—struggled to get the American medical community to focus attention on the syndrome and recognize that an organic agent was at work, even if it was an elusive one to find.

Meanwhile, the popular media, which had generally been promoting the idea that CFS was psychosomatic, began to reverse itself. Articles appeared in various high-circulation publications, including Johnson's in *Rolling Stone*, arguing for the existence of a genuine organic origin for the disease. Still, the mystery remained of what that origin *was*. There were lots of theories and growing concern, but there was simply no concrete answer.

Finally, the CDC was convinced that there was in fact one recognizable disease at work, even though no one could identify the cause. In 1988, the agency gave this mystery condition a name, "chronic fatigue syndrome," and created a general case definition. The definition stated that a patient receiving the CFS diagnosis must have had persistent fatigue for at least six months that could not be attributed to any other cause and must have at least eight of a very broad list of symptoms, including sleep disturbances and swollen or tender lymph nodes.

CFS Today

Over the next few years, CFS caught the attention of more members of the medical community. One researcher was quoted in *Newsweek* as calling CFS "the disease of the '90s"[6] because it seemed to be coming to the forefront of the public consciousness much as AIDS had captured the public's attention in the 1980s. And in a November 19, 1990, article, *Wall Street Journal* reporter Ron Winslow noted that the CDC was about to launch a study of CFS, writing that the study "represents the U.S. government's first major acknowledgment of the illness, a move that is long overdue in the view of many patients and researchers."[7]

As interest in CFS grew and more was learned about the disease, patients and doctors argued in favor of a more accurate and precise description from the CDC, one that reflected the emerging complexities of the disease. This revised definition was finally released by the CDC in 1994, and it remains the current basis for diagnosis. In order to receive a CFS diagnosis, a patient must have developed persistent and chronic fatigue that is not the direct result of exertion and is not helped by rest. The fatigue must also have produced a change in the patient's productivity levels in all major life spheres: work (or school, in the case of children), social, and personal. Along with this unrelenting fatigue, the CDC's criteria list eight other symptoms, stating that at least four of them need to be present along with fatigue for at least six months, but not be present before the onset of fatigue.

In spite of this more detailed case definition of CFS, there is no definite figure available of the current prevalence of CFS, for a variety of reasons. As Katrina Berne explains in *Chronic Fatigue Syndrome, Fibromyalgia and Other Invisible Illnesses: The Comprehensive Guide:* "Problems estimating the true prevalence of CFS include differing criteria; shifting case definitions; exclusion of children, the elderly, and those in remission; varying methods of collecting data; misdiagnosis with other disorders; and different prevalence rates in specific groups of individuals or geographic locations."[8] But various studies place the estimated number of individuals worldwide with the disease in the low millions, and experts say this number is continuing to grow.

Criteria of CFS

- Severe chronic fatigue lasting at least six months

- Four or more of the following symptoms:
    - Substantial impairment in short-term memory or concentration
    - Sore throat
    - Tender lymph nodes
    - Muscle pain
    - Multi-joint pain without swelling or redness
    - Headaches of a new type, pattern, or severity
    - Unrefreshing sleep
    - Post-exertional malaise lasting at least twenty-four hours

- Symptoms must have persisted or recurred during six or more consecutive months of illness and must not predate fatigue.

As Johnson predicted, CFS has been found across a wider range of ages and social classes than initially thought. When questioned about why so many of his patients were well-to-do people in their thirties and forties, Cheney pointed to the structure of the nation's health care system:

> Only people from higher socioeconomic groups, and highly educated people, have the ability to get through the roadblocks that exist to this diagnosis. It requires persistence, an ability to challenge medical authority. . . . I've received hundreds of letters from all over the country, and interestingly, the majority of those letters come from lower socioeconomic classes. . . . People without money write me because it's free. I think there are large numbers of people with this who are trapped. They're trapped by money problems, and by the inability to deal with the medical establishment as it perceives this disease.[9]

There have been no attempts to determine how many children have been stricken, as Berne mentions, but there has been ample evidence of the disease occurring in young people. Still, the disease is seen predominantly in people between the ages of twenty-five and fifty. Interestingly, it has been noted that while both genders are affected roughly equally in children, adult women are diagnosed at somewhere between twice and three times the rate of adult men, a disparity that doctors have not yet been able to explain.

Much has been learned about CFS in recent decades, but many questions remain. It has still not been proven whether CFS is a new disease or an old disease with a new name. But after years of unexplained symptoms and mysterious outbreaks, there is now at least a name and a definition for the condition that confronts millions of people today. And the official acknowledgment and identification of the syndrome is an important step as doctors attempt to make a diagnosis.

Chapter 2

Symptoms and Diagnosis

AFTER YEARS OF debate over whether doctors dealing with mysterious outbreaks across the country were all seeing evidence of one common disease, there was finally some consensus reached with the 1994 publication of the Centers for Disease Control and Prevention's (CDC) revised case definition of chronic fatigue syndrome (CFS). But even at this point, diagnosing CFS remained a problem for many reasons. Primarily, since the question of a cause was still unresolved, there was no single test to perform that could yield a clear positive or negative result for CFS. As Dr. David S. Bell explains: "The mark of modern medicine is to jump to the lab test that will give the answer in the least amount of time. . . . This approach simply does not work with the CFIDS patients."[10]

Even when a physician examines a patient while giving careful consideration to the CDC's criteria for diagnosis of CFS, obstacles remain to making that determination. "The CDC case definition is not always a useful tool for clinicians," argue Erica F. Verrillo and Lauren M. Gellman in their book *Chronic Fatigue Syndrome: A Treatment Guide*. "Unfortunately, a significant proportion of patients with CFIDS do not meet these rather rigid criteria."[11] Commenting further on the limitations of the CDC definition, Katrina Berne, an experienced clinician and CFS patient herself, explains that "criteria are assessed at only one point in time, based only on presence but not severity of symptoms. Individuals who do not have 'new or definite onset' (vague terms) are excluded. Symptoms must begin after the onset of fatigue, yet this is not always the case in CFS. . . . One perplexing flaw is the lack of definition for fatigue and an inability to assess it."[12] In other words, the case definition sets a certain standard that doctors have found does not always apply to all patients who fit the profile of a CFS patient, and at the same time the definition does not provide a way to measure the actual degree of symptoms, such as fatigue.

With all of these challenges facing a doctor attempting to determine if a patient has CFS, making the diagnosis depends heavily on an intense and subjective observation of symptoms on the part of the patient and doctor.

Symptoms

A focus on the symptoms of CFS can itself be complex, because there is a vast list of possible symptoms, and not every patient experiences every one or to the same degree of severity. But certain symptoms must be present before a doctor arrives at a CFS diagnosis. The first is extreme fatigue, to the point of near-constant exhaustion—not simple tiredness from physical activity or mental effort. As Greg Charles Fisher, who has suffered from CFS for years, explains: "CFS fatigue is to end-of-the-day tiredness what lightning is to a spark."[13] Furthermore, this fatigue does not improve with rest and is worsened by any kind of exertion. Accompanying this fatigue is often a feeling of malaise or general ill health and something patients and doctors call "brain fog," which results in the CFS sufferer having trouble concentrating and staying alert.

Other common symptoms resemble those of the flu, including sore throat, muscle weakness and joint pain, swollen or tender lymph nodes and low-grade fever. "After years of health, sound nutrition and a rigorous exercise regime, I was stricken quite suddenly with an ailment I decided was the flu," Hillary Johnson relates in her *Rolling Stone* article.

> Yet nearly a month passed without improvement. In fact, I was getting worse. . . . An appalling weakness, on most days, prevented me from walking. I soon was unable to stand long

enough to take a shower; my arm ached from the effort required to brush my teeth. My hand coordination seemed affected; I had difficulty picking up small objects. My head felt swathed in cotton.[14]

People with CFS also experience severe headaches that are different from any headaches they had in the past. These headaches often resemble migraine headaches, which cause nausea and sensitivity to light and noise along with pain. Some patients report a sensation of unrelenting pressure at the base of their skulls, or intense pain behind their eyes.

Numerous other symptoms are possible, involving—to name just some—sleep disturbances such as vivid nightmares and night sweats, panic and anxiety disorders, cardiac irregularities, skin problems such as rashes, abdominal pain and intestinal disorders such as irritable bowel syndrome, and bladder disturbances such as a frequent need to urinate and pain with urination.

There is a general, though not universal, pattern wherein patients are stricken first with fatigue and flu-like symptoms, the latter of which ease over time as other symptoms, particularly the cognitive difficulties, appear and become more disruptive.

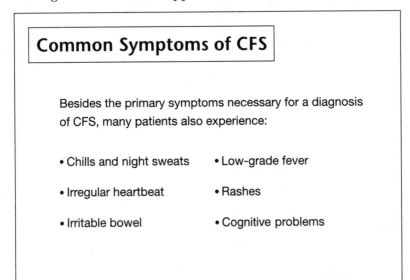

Common Symptoms of CFS

Besides the primary symptoms necessary for a diagnosis of CFS, many patients also experience:

• Chills and night sweats   • Low-grade fever

• Irregular heartbeat   • Rashes

• Irritable bowel   • Cognitive problems

Because there is such a broad range of possible symptoms, it sometimes takes patients and doctors longer to realize that all of the problems are connected to one another and part of a single disorder. "I was ill for many months before I realized that seemingly unrelated symptoms were part of the same disease,"[15] Johnson shares.

Symptoms in Children

If the symptoms of CFS in adults present a challenge to a physician attempting a diagnosis, they can be even more challenging when the victim is a child or adolescent. While CFS is diagnosed less frequently in children and adolescents—and is very rarely diagnosed in children under the age of eight—the disease also has a recognizable symptom pattern in young people. Children complain of flu-like symptoms that persist for much longer than a typical case of influenza; they report having headaches, fevers, swollen glands, upset stomachs, and pain and weakness in joints and muscles. "I was in such severe pain sometimes I would just lay there and cry, unable to move,"[16] shares Beth, who asked that her last name not be used, and who became sick at age thirteen. Most of the symptoms in children are similar to what adults experience, although there are some key differences. According to Bell:

> One striking difference is that in children the numerous symptoms appear to be almost equally severe. In adults it is common to hear that certain symptoms are always the most severe, but children may state that sore throat and headaches are the worst symptom one day, followed the next day by lymphatic and abdominal pain. This rotation in symptoms is frustrating [for a doctor attempting to make a diagnosis], for just when the pediatrician is about to begin an evaluation of the headaches, they may improve, replaced by joint pains as the most severe symptom.[17]

Adults and children with CFS also tend to experience the neurological and cognitive symptoms differently. Typically, these symptoms are less severe in children. However, even if the symptoms themselves are not as noticeable, their effect can be

CFS in Children

• Children most commonly report symptoms such as dizziness, sore throat, abdominal pain, headache, fever, and swollen glands.

• In most children, particularly adolescents, symptoms appear suddenly, within a few days or weeks.

• In younger children, symptoms appear gradually, over several months or longer.

more severe in someone whose mind is still developing. As Bell explains: "Adults have a clear perception of their abilities, so that memory loss and inability to concentrate are easily recognized. Children are less sure of their abilities, and these symptoms manifest as progressive school difficulties."[18] In other words, children and adolescents with CFS might not report confusion or problems with memory loss and brain fog, because they do not even realize these problems are abnormal; they often attribute their difficulties to a lack of intelligence. Because their patients may not notice or report such symptoms, pediatricians must look for signs such as slipping grades and overall decreased success in school to discern the cognitive problems that signify CFS.

Another Explanation?

CFS symptoms can be found in a variety of other disorders, all of which need to be carefully ruled out since effective treatment depends on accurate diagnosis. When confronted with a patient—either adult or child—reporting a constellation of symptoms resembling those of CFS, a doctor's first step is to eliminate the possibility of other diseases that could also cause these symptoms.

Depending on a particular patient's overall health picture, family history, symptoms, and initial test results, doctors might check for a variety of conditions in adults: rheumatoid arthritis, allergies, a malignancy (particularly lymphoma), fibromyalgia, multiple sclerosis, multiple chemical sensitivity disorder, systemic lupus erythematosus, or a mental illness such as depression or panic disorder. They might also look for an infectious disease, such as Lyme disease, and/or a chronic inflammatory disease, such as sarcoidosis.

The list of alternative diagnoses is just as long among children, although there are some differences in the conditions that top the list. Since gastrointestinal symptoms are often more severe in children, pediatricians must consider and eliminate intestinal diseases such as Crohn's Disease, celiac disease, and ulcerative colitis. These illnesses can affect adults as well as children, but typically an adult with CFS does not report the same type of gastrointestinal symptoms that a child with CFS does. Food allergies, attention deficit disorder, and childhood migraine syndrome might also be considered in children.

A nurse administers an allergy test in an effort to determine the cause of a patient's symptoms.

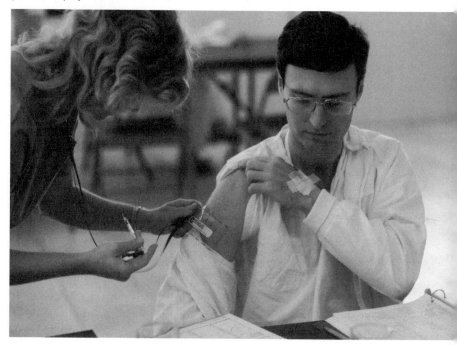

Finally, the rotation of symptoms such as a throbbing headache one day and achy joints another may indicate that the illness is simply the result of emotional distress caused by school phobia (fear of school) or separation anxiety disorder (extreme fear of being away from one or both parents).

Making the Diagnosis

Diagnosing CFS can be a complicated and daunting task, due to the long list of symptoms and numerous possible explanations for those symptoms. But it is possible to make the diagnosis; it just takes a good deal of persistence and effort on the part of both the doctor and the patient. Many patients report having waited years to receive a diagnosis and visiting multiple physicians before finding one who identifies the problem.

Of course, part of the reason a CFS diagnosis can take so long is that excluding other possibilities is complicated and involves many different tests, some of which are painful and can be expensive. Meanwhile, waiting for results from such tests can be extremely stressful and frightening for the patient. "Like a teenager awaiting a prom invitation, I sat near the telephone waiting to hear whether I had a brain tumor, hypoglycemia, heart problems, multiple sclerosis, or an ulcer," Berne relates. "Initial relief at knowing what I *didn't* have was quickly replaced with fear of not knowing what I *did* have."[19] Complicating the diagnostic process further is the fact that some of the disorders with similar symptoms are *themselves* diagnosed by excluding other possibilities, since these conditions also do not yet have effective diagnostic tests. Furthermore, since it is possible that a patient suffers from more than one disease, a diagnosis of a different disease does not absolutely rule out the possibility that the patient suffers from CFS as well.

Of course, a thorough study of the symptoms plays the most important role in diagnosing any illness. What complicates diagnosing CFS still further is that so many of its symptoms lack objective descriptions. For instance, the degree of exhaustion can be affected by how patients *perceive* their own feelings. Two people might both use the word "exhausted" to describe how tired they feel, but they could mean it in different ways. Whereas one patient considers himself exhausted if he can only finish one mile of his daily three-mile run, another patient's exhaustion might keep her from engaging in any strenuous physical activity at all. Even this difference has to be looked at in the context of an individual's lifestyle; the fact that one person is capable of less physical activity than another does not necessarily mean that only one of these two patients has CFS. Moreover, not every CFS patient is totally incapacitated by the illness.

For this reason, doctors need to obtain a full patient health history in order to understand what the reported symptoms mean both objectively and within each patient's life. It is cru-

Yawning, a student suffering from CFS attempts to pay attention in class. Some people diagnosed with CFS are still capable of keeping up with some daily activities.

cial that doctors get the clearest picture they can of how each patient's ability to function has been impaired. As Bell explains: "The physician must return to sound clinical medicine, taking a complete medical history and listening to the entire range of symptoms in order to observe the underlying pattern."[20] In practical terms, this means spending more time with a patient—and time is something that modern physicians do not have in abundance.

Given the reality that doctors are often rushed, the patient must take extra care to offer a detailed health history. This can pose its own set of challenges, since not all patients can remember or communicate every important detail of their illness. Along with giving a specific and in-depth impression of the symptoms themselves, patients can help doctors with their account of how and when they became sick.

Unlike many chronic diseases, CFS is often characterized by abrupt onset, meaning the patient can pin down an exact moment when he or she became ill. This is not always true, however, as recent research has revealed that on reflection, many patients can recall a period of mild weakness or other symptoms leading up to the onset of severe illness. But the ability to identify an abrupt downswing into being very sick, very suddenly, supports a diagnosis of CFS, which is why the factor of "new or definite onset" of fatigue is even included in the CDC's definition of the syndrome.

Yet, frustratingly, CFS does not strike everyone suddenly. In particular, while older adolescents tend, like adults, to develop symptoms abruptly, younger patients—those who have not yet gone through puberty—usually develop the disease more gradually. For these young patients, doctors focus more on the presence of a range of symptoms typical in children with CFS, such as recurrent sore throat, muscle pain, headache, and abdominal pain.

To make the diagnosis in children, doctors must also exclude the other possible causes of symptoms as they would do with an adult patient. Again, the children's reports of symptoms, severity, and timing are crucial to this process. It can be even more difficult, however, for physicians to receive an accurate and full-symptom report from children than from adults. Often, doctors rely heavily on observations made by parents and teachers and noticeable changes in behavior to supplement a child's own description of the problem.

Because children with CFS usually notice different symptoms from day to day, pediatricians often give special consideration to alternative explanations for symptoms, such as school phobia and separation anxiety disorder. Bell, for one, suggests that it is easy to rule out the former of these two: "In school phobia, children do not want to go to school . . . and they will invent ways to avoid it. Therefore, because of the anxiety about going to school, a child might have a stomachache and not 'feel well' at 7:30 on a school-day morning. But these complaints are never expressed in the afternoon, when school is over, or on Saturday morning."[21] On the other hand, a child suffering from CFS will feel too exhausted to leave bed whether the destination is school or a desirable location such as an amusement park. Other experts note that the method of excluding separation anxiety disorder is basically the same. Verrillo and Gellman say, for example, "[c]hildren with separation anxiety display symptoms when anticipating separation but which resolve when separation does not occur."[22] However, children with CFS will complain of symptoms such as headaches and sore throats whether their parents are leaving their side or not.

Supporting a Diagnosis

When the symptoms fit the accepted pattern for the patient's age group and last for at least six months, and when other possible explanations have been eliminated, a knowledgeable doctor can make the diagnosis of CFS. Also, while no test can *diagnose* CFS, there are studies emerging that suggest certain abnormal lab results can *support* a diagnosis, because these results have been found commonly in patients believed to have CFS. For instance, people with CFS tend to test positive for certain types of viral infections, including cytomegalovirus, Epstein-Barr virus, human herpesvirus 6, and Coxsackie virus. Their bodies also often react unusually to physical exercise. Studies have found that, unlike in healthy individuals, CFS patients' levels of the stress hormone cortisol will drop after exercise and cerebral blood flow will decrease. Furthermore, while the ability of a normal person's body to utilize glucose improves after exercise, this is not usually the case for someone with CFS. Finally, there are some specific abnormalities found with the immune system function of CFS patients, including low levels of

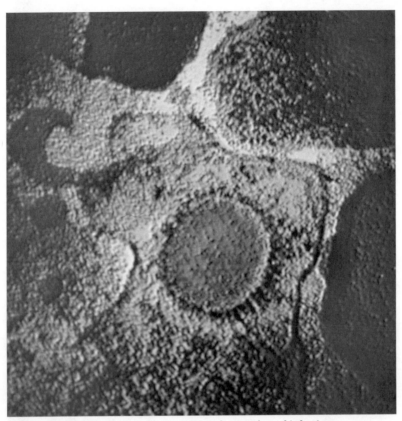

A cell infected with cytomegalovirus, one of a number of infections common among CFS patients.

natural killer cells, which are specialized blood cells that are the first line of defense against viruses and other invaders to the body.

The diagnostic process for CFS tends to be a long and complicated one, and patients often experience a degree of relief after finally hearing an answer to what is wrong. However, the challenges and complications a CFS patient faces do not end after receiving a diagnosis.

Chapter 3

Problems and Complications

W HILE THERE ARE certain prominent symptoms of chronic fatigue syndrome (CFS) that help a doctor make the diagnosis, CFS patients often experience many problems beyond these symptoms. These problems are varied and can include further physical health complications and also emotional and practical difficulties that accompany the lifestyle changes people with CFS are often forced to make.

Possible Health Complications

The most debilitating symptoms of CFS are often not among the first to appear. After the initial period of fatigue, pain, headaches, and flu-like symptoms, numerous further complications can develop, the most devastating being the potentially severe cognitive impairments. According to Erica F. Verrillo and Lauren M. Gellman, "Loss of concentration is one of the most common—and serious—cognitive problems affecting people with [CFS]. . . . The brain lags and either processes new information slowly or misses it entirely."[23]

Everyday activities become burdensome. People with CFS often lose the ability to keep up with a conversation because they have extreme trouble focusing on what the other person is saying and processing the meaning of the words. Reading becomes a slow, laborious process because a patient might have to read one sentence many times in order to really grasp its meaning. "I couldn't concentrate to read, and when I did, the words leaped all over the page," Hillary Johnson says of her worst days. "I was unable to hold a conversation with more than one person. When I spoke, I often used words entirely inappropriate to the meaning of my sentence; I forgot my subject in midstream. I also forgot the names of friends, common household words and the names of schools I had attended."[24] Driving even on short errands may be risky; a CFS sufferer might not stop at a red light in time because it can take too long to respond to the signal by moving one's foot from the accelerator to the brake pedal.

Not only do CFS patients have trouble processing information, they also have problems retaining it. Memory loss, particularly short-term memory loss, is another common cognitive complication of CFS. Patients often describe forgetting people's names or the words for various common objects. They frequently have trouble remembering what they were just doing or were about to do, and why. Multitasking—that is, the handling of more than one task at once—becomes a real challenge because CFS limits one's ability to focus on even one task. Daily chores requiring basic math skills, such as balancing a checkbook, often become so demanding that a person with CFS can no longer complete them without assistance.

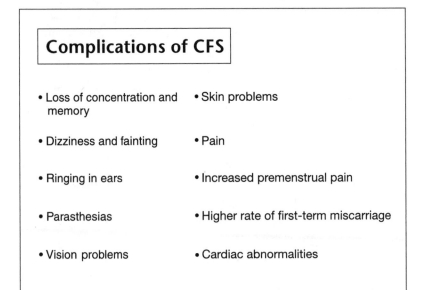

Complications of CFS

- Loss of concentration and memory

- Dizziness and fainting

- Ringing in ears

- Parasthesias

- Vision problems

- Skin problems

- Pain

- Increased premenstrual pain

- Higher rate of first-term miscarriage

- Cardiac abnormalities

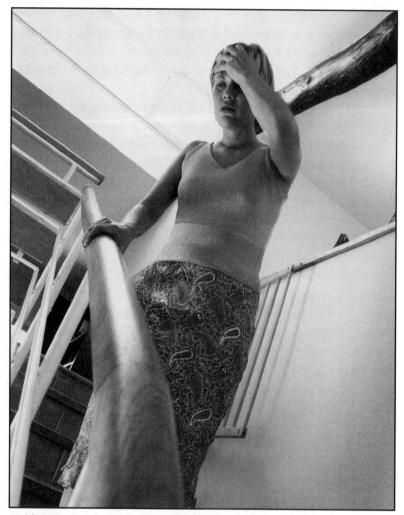

Holding the handrail, a woman suffers from dizziness, which is often associated with CFS.

The possible neurological symptoms and complications extend beyond cognitive function and also involve motor skills and balance. Recalls John (who asked that his last name not be used) of the early day of his illness, "When I tried to stand up, my legs felt like rubber. My head pounded and I was dizzy and nauseous."[25] Patients often experience dizziness and even fainting spells, a ringing in their ears, and paresthesias, a condition involving numbness, shooting pains, or a burning, tingling sensation in the extremities. "Some patients have burning sensations in the fingers to the degree that they are unable to hold a pencil,"[26] Dr. David S. Bell relates. In rare cases, seizures or seizure-like episodes can occur.

These neurological problems are often worsened by accompanying problems with vision. People with CFS sometimes have a high sensitivity to light, meaning that normal levels of indoor lighting or sunlight outdoors appear much brighter, becoming nearly blinding and sometimes causing pain. They also report blind spots, blurred vision, and dryness, burning, and pain in their eyes, or even "floaters," meaning black spots that seem to float in front of their eyes.

Virtually every organ is affected by CFS. Dry skin is another frequent problem, along with other skin conditions such as rashes, eczema, redness, and thinning of hair. Sometimes CFS patients actually lose clearly defined fingerprints, due to atrophy of the skin on their fingertips.

Pain remains a central reality for sufferers of CFS as the disease progresses, although it sometimes develops in new areas of the body. For instance, people with CFS sometimes begin to feel pain and a burning sensation when they urinate, along with feeling the need to urinate more frequently. Though these can be symptoms of a bladder infection, most often the patient with CFS who experiences these problems does not actually have an infection, so there is no quick treatment to ease symptoms. Sometimes, the problem becomes chronic, developing into a condition called interstitial cystitis. In these cases, patients must experiment with methods to manage the pain such as over-the-counter pain relievers and certain prescription drugs.

Women, who suffer disproportionately higher from CFS than men, often face an increase in premenstrual pain; their CFS symptoms in general also tend to worsen during menstruation. In addition, CFS sufferers seem to be at a higher risk of first-trimester miscarriages than the rest of the population.

Certain cardiovascular problems appear to affect both men and women with CFS more frequently than the general population. Increased heart rate, palpitations, and a faint murmur attributed to the common and fairly minor condition called mitral valve prolapse are all problems that doctors see with greater frequency among CFS patients than in the population at large. More serious cardiac complications are rare but have been seen, and many doctors report an apparently low blood volume, a potentially major complication, in CFS patients.

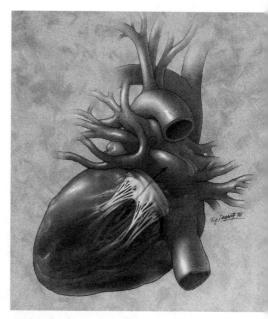

In this illustration of the heart, an arrow shows where blood leaks backward into the atrium as a result of mitral valve prolapse.

Associated Diseases

Of course, being diagnosed with an illness such as CFS does not preclude the possibility of developing some other illness. In fact, sometimes even the opposite can be true: Having certain conditions can make someone *more* likely to develop other specific diseases. When this happens, the diseases are called "associated diseases." And there are several conditions that appear to be associated with CFS.

Most common of the associated conditions is allergies. The majority of people diagnosed with CFS either experience a worsening of existing allergies or develop new ones. "Many patients who had childhood allergies and were free of them for years develop allergies again when they become ill with CFIDS," Bell observes. "And some patients who have never had allergies at all will develop them after becoming ill."[27] Since allergies result from an immune system that is responding inappropriately to substances that are usually harmless, such as pollen or peanuts, some doctors

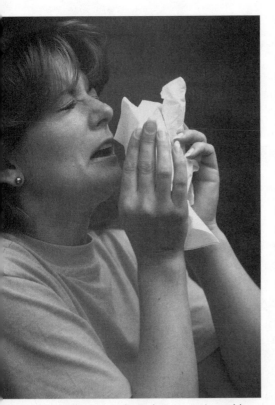

Allergies such as those experienced by this patient are commonly associated with CFS.

wonder if the association between CFS and allergies points to the role of a faulty, overactive immune system in CFS. However, this question has yet to be answered.

While many experts remain intrigued by the association with allergies, researchers tend to focus most on understanding the exact relationship between CFS and a second associated condition: fibromyalgia, a disease for which there is also no known cause or cure, and which shares many symptoms and complications with CFS. The primary difference between the two disorders is that while CFS was named for its hallmark symptom of extreme fatigue, the predominant symptom of fibromyalgia is not exhaustion but pain throughout the whole body, particularly in certain areas of the body called "tender spots." Some experts speculate that CFS and fibromyalgia are variations of the same illness; indeed, most books available on either disease address *both* conditions together. Treatment manuals, in particular, do so since the treatments that have been successful for symptoms of CFS are also given to patients with fibromyalgia. "[CFS and fibromyalgia] share the same common symptoms, demographics, sleep physiology, and abnormalities in neurological, immune system, and endocrine function,"[28] Katrina Berne writes. A difficulty in achieving deep, restorative sleep appears to lie at the heart of both illnesses, and patients with either or both diseases report the same strange sensitivities to light, sound, and changes in temperature, along with experiencing a similar range of cognitive, cardiac, gastrointestinal, skin, bladder, and other problems.

Despite these overlaps between CFS and fibromyalgia, there are some key differences that lead to a diagnosis of one or the other, and that can even lead to someone being diagnosed with both. The first difference, of course, is in the predominant symptoms of fatigue and pain, respectively. Also, although many of the symptoms are shared, the severity of certain symptoms seems to distinguish the two diseases. Doctors who study the type of pain caused by fibromyalgia are called rheumatologists, and it was the American College of Rheumatology that established the criteria for a diagnosis of fibromyalgia, released in 1990. To receive the diagnosis, a patient must report having experienced widespread chronic pain for at least three months, and, most importantly, must experience pain when pressure is applied to at least eleven of the eighteen areas of the body identified as tender points by rheumatologists.

Just how fibromyalgia is connected to CFS is still a subject of debate. In the meantime, however, many patients with CFS must also cope with the more severe pain of fibromyalgia and adjust their treatments and lifestyles accordingly.

The Role of Depression

If the connection between CFS and fibromyalgia is complex, still more complicated is the relationship between CFS and depression. People with CFS often express various emotions related to depression, including despair, hopelessness, and helplessness. They may lose interest in things that once brought them pleasure or withdraw from people around them. The high rate of depression among CFS patients, combined with the inability to pinpoint an organic cause for the disease, has led various researchers to suggest that CFS is in fact a symptom of depression.

Such a relationship is at least plausible, since it is not unheard of for severe emotional problems to cause physical symptoms. Experts, however, widely reject this theory for several reasons. For one thing, the depression experienced by CFS patients occurs *after* onset of their physical symptoms, not before. For this reason, depression is widely believed to be a symptom or complication, rather than a cause, of CFS. "The symptoms of primary depression are quite dissimilar to the symptoms of CFIDS patients," Bell explains. "While up to 60 percent of [CFS] patients are depressed, 40 percent are not, or have only minimal depression expected from the life disruption they experience. Emotionally healthy children develop CFIDS and have less depression than adults in the first few years of the illness. And ... if CFIDS is a mental illness, why does it occur in epidemics?"[29]

Diagnosed with severe depression, a young man is also thought to suffer from CFS.

Those who believe that depression is not a cause of CFS offer multiple explanations for the high number of CFS patients who suffer from depression. The first is simple: Being sick in itself can be depressing. In support of this, Hillary Johnson describes her initial period of illness the following way: "I felt as if I had tumbled into a deep, dark hole and was spinning, head over heels, into blackness."[30] Depression commonly accompanies chronic illness of all types, experts argue. And some ask rhetorically whether a cancer patient would be told he or she did not have cancer just because he or she was also depressed, or if he or she would be told that the cancer was caused by depression.

The source of the depression, most experts say, is clear. Beyond the frustration over being physically ill, people with CFS often experience difficulty accepting limitations that they feel define them in the eyes of their peers. Although no direct causal link has been established, research does indicate that a large portion of adult CFS patients were once highly driven, ambitious, and hard-working people who squeezed as much into their days as possible. After becoming ill, this level of activity is usually no longer possible. For someone who once defined him- or herself through a certain level of productivity at work, this can be devastating. As Greg Charles Fisher relates: "It is not easy to be seen as helpless in a society that prides itself on its go-it-alone mentality."[31] Along with a significant decrease in energy levels, some patients also face the deterioration of cognitive abilities, leaving them entirely unable to perform tasks that were once central to their lives and careers.

In a culture that promotes independence and the "superman/woman" model of someone who can do and have it all, there is a double blow because patients feel that they are letting down both themselves and others around them. One patient was

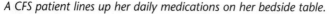

A CFS patient lines up her daily medications on her bedside table.

crushed by the change in his role in both the workforce and within his family. "I was always the go-to guy," he shared, "and now I couldn't even take care of myself."[32]

CFS patients can also become depressed from the challenges of modifying their social and personal lives to accommodate their disease. Just as they often have to cut back on hours at work or even quit their jobs altogether, people with CFS also have limited energy and stamina for pleasurable activities. A young, single person might encounter difficulties in dating, for example, while parents often feel they are not able to do enough with their children. "You become a different person,"[33] says Jon Sterling, chairman of the board of the CFIDS Association of America. Sterling says he had barely missed a day of work in twenty years before his illness, and he had tremendous difficulty facing the fact that he had to quit his job and retire on disability insurance.

Just as adults often define themselves in terms of their work and find CFS particularly challenging for that reason, children and teenagers with CFS can easily become depressed about how their lives came to differ from those of their peers. They might face a change in their performance in school, or have to miss a great deal of school, as well as lose out on time with friends and important social events such as dances or parties. A child or teen with ambitious goals can become frustrated and depressed when this illness stands in the way. "Despite being an honors student [prior to becoming sick] . . . the school pushed me to go into regular classes," Beth shares. "When I was in high school and wanted to take Advanced Placement courses, they tried to refuse, despite my having all the qualifications and skills."[34] The school's reluctance was rooted in the fact that Beth had to complete her work from home as she was too sick to attend the actual classes. She finally won the right to remain in the higher-level classes, but in order to keep up with her workload she worked with tutors year-round, seven days a week. This kind of grueling and isolating experience can easily take its toll on the emotions of a young person.

Financial Struggles

For many adults with CFS, the greatest practical challenge is their inability to work as much as they did previously (if at all) and the serious financial strain this places on them. Typically, people who develop chronic illnesses can apply for and receive long-term disability benefits from the government. However, the remaining controversy over cause, diagnosis, and even the very existence of CFS makes the application process for disability payments more complicated. Patients who feel unable to work must seek the assistance of their physicians and often members of a local or national support group to help them collect benefits. Also, some patients recover to different degrees over time, making the decision of who is truly too sick to work—and for how long—especially tricky. Even after an initial qualification for disability payments, CFS patients are often required to undergo repeated evaluation.

In addition to traditional health and disability benefits, other kinds of help are now becoming available for patients who need it. More and more people are becoming aware of the many physical, emotional, and lifestyle complications that affect someone with CFS, and attention is increasingly given to ways of dealing with these problems along with treating the primary symptoms of the disease. But the real key to being able to address all of the symptoms, effects, and complications of CFS lies in uncovering the answer to the most important question of what, exactly, causes the disease.

Chapter 4

The Question of a Cause

AS RESEARCHERS LOOK for a disease's cause, one of the first questions they need to answer is whether the disease is contagious, and if so, how it is being spread. For example, epidemiologists will try to determine if the disease can be passed through casual contact or through the exchange of bodily fluids. Since over the years chronic fatigue syndrome (CFS) has appeared to strike clusters of people, there was a strong fear at one point that the disease was contagious. But on closer examination, evidence so far does not support this theory, since many spouses and family members of CFS patients remain healthy, as do others who come into contact with these patients. Instead, some experts suggest that the people infected in these outbreaks were all exposed to a common causative agent, an agent that has yet to be identified.

A Virus?

There are plenty of theories regarding possible causes of CFS. One of the earliest and most widely supported theories holds that CFS is caused by a virus. Viruses are so tiny that they are invisible even under all but the most powerful microscopes, so the most common way to detect them is to test for antibodies that the body develops in response to a viral infection. However, a positive test for a particular antibody does not mean someone has an active infection. A person will test positive for these antibodies after only having been *exposed* to a virus. Therefore, a positive test for a virus does not necessarily prove that this organism is causing whatever symptoms a patient is showing.

In the case of CFS, Epstein-Barr virus is an excellent example of the difficulty of establishing a causal relationship. It is estimated that nearly every person who reaches adulthood is exposed to Epstein-Barr at some point and will develop the corresponding antibodies. This is why Drs. Daniel Peterson's and Paul Cheney's findings that the majority of their patients in Incline Village had high levels of antibodies to the Epstein-Barr virus were not viewed as meaningful by the Centers for Disease Control and Prevention. In the opinion of many experts, *any* group of adults could have tested positive for Epstein-Barr, regardless of their state of health.

In fact, even though much of the early focus was on the Epstein-Barr virus as a possible cause of CFS, researchers have considered other viruses as suspects as well. Elevated levels of antibodies for cytomegalovirus, human herpesvirus 6, herpes simplex, rubella, and Coxsackie have all been found in the blood of many CFS patients. And some experts continue to suspect that a different form of the polio virus causes CFS. Still others wonder if CFS will turn out to be caused by an as-yet unidentified virus.

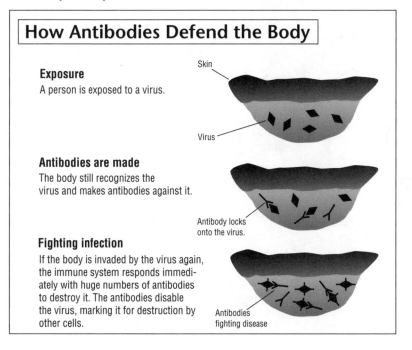

How Antibodies Defend the Body

Exposure
A person is exposed to a virus.

Skin

Virus

Antibodies are made
The body still recognizes the virus and makes antibodies against it.

Antibody locks onto the virus.

Fighting infection
If the body is invaded by the virus again, the immune system responds immediately with huge numbers of antibodies to destroy it. The antibodies disable the virus, marking it for destruction by other cells.

Antibodies fighting disease

There is also a possibility that a long-dormant virus is some-how reactivated to cause the symptoms of CFS. Of course, if a long-dormant virus suddenly comes to life, the question is: What is causing the renewed activity of the virus in the system?

One expert, Katrina Berne, suggests that this renewed activity could be the result of an impaired immune system that can in turn have a number of causes:

> Nonviral triggering factors that interfere with immune func-tioning may allow viruses to move from dormant to active states so that viral activation is an effect, rather than a cause, of illness. The cause may turn out to be a newly discovered virus, a more virulent strain of a known virus, a recombinant virus, a faulty immune system reacting inappropriately to a "normal" virus, all of the above—or none of the above.[35]

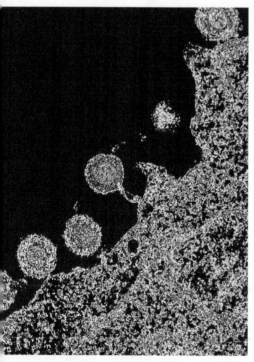

Human herpesvirus 6 infects a cell, causing the cell to produce more of the virus.

As Berne's comment sug-gests, exactly what role viruses play in the cause of CFS re-mains obscure. But some ex-perts interpret the fact that CFS patients often test positive for numerous viruses as sug-gesting that a separate factor is leaving the body vulnerable to these viruses, most likely a problem with the body's im-mune system.

Immune Dysfunction

Strong evidence exists that a malfunction of the immune system plays a large part in this illness, though once again researchers have not been able to pinpoint the reasons for and nature of the malfunction. In fact, scientists have actually seen two *opposite* problems at once: both an over- and underactivity of the immune system of a CFS patient. Dr. David S. Bell notes that the apparent abnormality of the immune response is what prompts some experts to use the phrase "chronic fatigue immune dysfunction syndrome" as an alternate and preferred name for this disorder.

Some studies have in fact shown lower levels of the immune system's disease-fighting cells, known as natural killer cells, in patients with CFS. However, researchers can only speculate as to what causes the immune system to weaken. Some scientists have explored the possibility that one of a special class of viruses—a retrovirus—is the culprit, but so far they have been unable to find strong evidence to support this theory.

Another theory regarding the cause of the immune suppression in CFS patients is an overgrowth of yeast in the body, a condition called systemic candidiasis. This is one of the more controversial theories, accepted as possible by practitioners of alternative medicine but given little credence by the mainstream medical community. Dr. Jacob Teitelbaum in his book *From Fatigued to Fantastic!*, a treatment manual for patients, explains the theory: "Yeast are normal members of the body's 'zoo.' They live in balance with bacteria—some of which are helpful and healthy, and some of which are detrimental and unhealthy. The problems begin when this harmonious balance shifts and the yeast begin to overgrow."[36] Teitelbaum explains that this yeast overgrowth can be caused by various factors, the most common being frequent antibiotic use. Antibiotics kill both good and bad bacteria in the body, he says. Teitelbaum goes on to argue that many doctors believe yeast overgrowth can cause suppression of the immune system.

The more widely accepted view, however, is that the overgrowth of yeast is an effect, not a cause, of immune dysfunction. Bell argues that "the presence of candidiasis is a sign of poor immune functioning, not just infection with yeast."[37] Still other experts prefer to withhold judgment. Berne, for example, says that "yeast overgrowth may be a causal contributor or a secondary effect of the illness, or both may be attributable to immune dysfunction."[38]

A related problem that Teitelbaum and practitioners of alternative medicine point to is bowel parasites, which they say can also suppress the immune system. Burton Goldberg, author of *Alternative Medicine Guide to Chronic Fatigue, Fibromyalgia and Environmental Illness*, notes that both candidiasis and bowel parasites are often present in people with CFS.

Even as many researchers focus on immune system suppression, others are looking at the evidence of overactivity in the immune system of CFS patients. An overactive immune system is one that is hyperaware of every seemingly "foreign" presence in the body, launching multiple attacks on perceived invaders. Some researchers suggest that CFS is the result of the immune system's overreaction to an infection of some kind and that the immune system continues its response even when the "invader" has been subdued. In this scenario, the symptoms of CFS would actually be caused by the body's own prolonged defenses against something that is no longer a threat. Along these lines, some experts wonder if CFS is actually what is known as an autoimmune disease, a class of diseases whereby the immune system treats parts of its own body as foreign and so the body attacks *itself*. The high ratio of adult women to adult men with CFS lends support to this theory, since a similar disparity between genders is found in most autoimmune diseases. Yet once again, the particular mechanism of how this autoimmune malfunction happens eludes detection, leaving the ideas of both immune suppression and immune system overactivity as possible ties to the cause of CFS, but not the definite answer at this point.

Hormones

Just as various abnormalities have been found with the immune systems of people with CFS, many of these patients also display irregularities in a part of the endocrine system known as the hypothalamic-pituitary-adrenal (HPA) axis, irregularities that might even be *linked* to the immune disturbances. Together, the hypothalamus and the pituitary and adrenal glands are responsible for a host of functions, such as controlling the body's appetite and temperature, helping the body's metabolism run smoothly, and

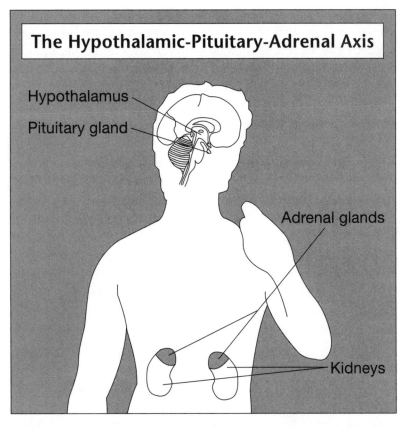

The Hypothalamic-Pituitary-Adrenal Axis

Hypothalamus

Pituitary gland

Adrenal glands

Kidneys

regulating the body's response to any kind of stress. These functions are accomplished through the various hormones secreted by the glands. Erica F. Verrillo and Lauren M. Gellman explain one possible connection between the endocrine and immune systems, stating that "the continued release of stress hormones leads to depression of the immune system, paving the way for opportunistic infections and increasing susceptibility to a host of transmissible diseases."[39]

There is certainly no question that when the delicate balance of the HPA axis is disturbed, and either too much or too little of the different hormones are released, the system is easily thrown into chaos; a person's ability to sleep, respond to pain, and even think clearly can all be affected. Because CFS patients often display abnormalities in these areas, researchers have investigated whether disturbances of the HPA axis could be behind the symptoms of CFS.

In fact, studies have shown that CFS patients often have numerous abnormal levels of the hormones produced and regulated by the HPA axis. People with CFS, for example, seem to have low levels of growth hormone, which is necessary for maintaining a person's energy and vitality. Patients also tend to have low levels of the related dehydroepiandrosterone hormone, a building block for the sex hormones estrogen and testosterone and also key to a functioning metabolism; low levels of cortisol, which also provides energy and aids in metabolism and coping with stressful situations; and decreased levels of thyroid hormone, which regulates body temperature and energy levels, among other functions. Some researchers have claimed that hypothyroidism itself could be the cause of CFS. According to Goldberg, "A major and often overlooked cause of chronic fatigue syndrome is . . . hypothyroidism. Although, according to practitioners of conventional medicine, hypothyroidism is a separate illness from CFS and a diagnosis of one precludes a diagnosis of the other, many people with CFS have not been properly tested for thyroid problems."[40] Goldberg maintains that hypothyroidism could easily be responsible by itself for many CFS symptoms, including low energy levels, mental sluggishness, memory disturbances, skin problems, and a lower tolerance for pain.

Other researchers attach special significance to the lower levels of cortisol found often in CFS patients. Cortisol, a hormone secreted by the adrenal glands, is responsible for providing energy and mental alertness. Levels of cortisol typically remain at relatively steady levels in healthy individuals, rising slightly higher in the morning hours and dropping at night. These levels rise dramatically, however, in response to physical or emotional stress, and with the dramatic rise comes a surge of energy. This process is called the "fight-or-flight" response, because its biological purpose is to help prepare someone to either deal with or flee immediate, life-threatening danger. However, the modern world is full of *non*-life-threatening stress that can trigger this response. Some researchers claim to have found that people with CFS tend to overreact to these more minor stimuli, with their bodies producing abnormally high levels of cortisol in response. In turn, the researchers speculate, this leads to *depleted* levels of cortisol on a daily basis when normal levels of the hormone are needed for energy because the adrenal glands become exhausted from repeated, unnecessary stimulation. "Whereas short bursts of stress hormones can be beneficial and, indeed, may be crucial in circumstances in which running from danger will guarantee survival," Verrillo and Gellman explain, "the long-term results [of frequent short bursts] can be disastrous."[41]

While there is evidence to support the theory that hormonal disturbances are important in CFS, once again the underlying question of what causes these disturbances remains unanswered, leaving researchers mystified as to whether endocrine abnormalities are the underlying cause of CFS or merely part of a more complex chain of events that originates outside the body altogether.

Environmental Factors

Some people have latched on to the idea of an overused fight-or-flight response and cited it as support for the theory that CFS is actually a result of the many evils of modern society, of which increased daily stress is just one. Echoing Dr. George M. Beard's concept of neurasthenia, some researchers claim that the pressures and developments of modern civilization are actually causing the breakdowns in people's bodies that lead to the illness of CFS. Other experts point to environmental factors, such as industrial pollutants and pesticides, exposure to which—just as hormonal disturbances can do—can cause

Some experts believe that smoke and other industrial pollutants play a role in CFS.

impairment to the immune system. Goldberg considers this theory a valid possibility and makes the point that people are exposed to chemicals in far greater concentrations today than in previous generations. He goes on to discuss problems with air and water quality, and all of the chemicals and pesticides allowed in the food supply, offering this evidence as support for the theory that CFS is a modern disease that can be blamed on these factors. Goldberg, however, is in the minority. While some experts acknowledge that chemicals and pollutants may play a role in CFS, most doctors reject chemical exposure as the primary cause of the disease.

Psychosomatic?

The fact that doctors and researchers have so far been unable to uncover the organic cause of CFS has led some observers to maintain that earlier opinions of CFS as being psychosomatic could have been on the mark, or at least close. These people point to the high incidence of depression among CFS patients and suggest that CFS is actually psychological in nature, that the patient's own brain conjures and creates symptoms that feel real. Someone with a psychosomatic illness can be just as sick as someone with a disease that has an organic cause; the key difference is that there is no external causative agent, such as a microbe, at work in a psychosomatic illness.

Although a small contingent of the medical community still believes that CFS is psychosomatic, doctors overwhelmingly believe there is more to CFS than psychology. They maintain that there is far too much evidence suggesting organic agents at work, even if these exact mechanisms have yet to be determined.

Searching for a Trigger

As researchers try to unravel the mystery of what causes CFS, some wonder what role, if any, genetics plays in determining who gets the disease. There is evidence that CFS can run in families, appearing particularly in first-degree relatives—that is, parents and siblings of the patient. However, no genetic marker has been identified, and the history of CFS being found in "clusters" of people who are not related argues strongly against a purely genetic cause. Researchers wonder instead if certain people are genetically predisposed to developing CFS, particularly when circumstances act as a trigger.

The idea is that whatever the underlying cause is, the onset of symptoms is the result of some sort of triggering event. This theory is supported by the fact that although they may later recall experiencing various mild ailments prior to the onset of major symptoms, many CFS patients can identify the precise moment they became ill. Many patients are able to describe a stressful emotional and/or physical experience that occurred right before they became sick, such as a car accident or minor surgery; others report an initial viral infection that ballooned into CFS. "I was hit by a car while riding my bike," one patient recalls. "And I just never recovered from the accident. Instead, I kept getting worse. A year and a half later, when I could barely walk, I was diagnosed with chronic fatigue syndrome."[42] Beth, another CFS patient, went into the hospital for routine surgery at age thirteen, and spent the next five years homebound and mostly bedridden from her symptoms. Bell lists a number of apparent triggers that he has seen in his patients: "exposure to certain chemicals, bacterial infections, emotional stress, surgical procedures, physical injury, immunizations, and physical stress."[43] Bell and others speculate that these trigger events could interact with other organic factors, including perhaps a genetic predisposition, to produce an active case of CFS.

A Combination of Factors

The fact is that no one theory accounts for all cases of CFS, yet all are supported by some evidence. Because of this, many experts are convinced that many factors work together to cause CFS. As Katrina Berne offers, "The many hypotheses [about the cause of CFS] are not mutually exclusive; many of them fit together well. Several factors may be involved: one to set the stage, one to ignite the fuse, and others to perpetuate the process [of getting sick]."[44]

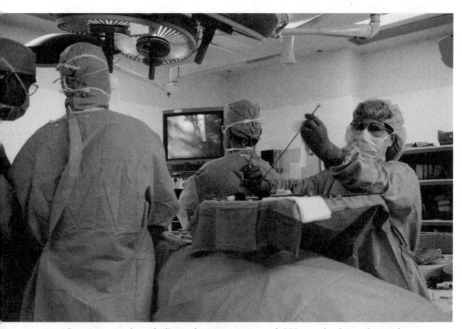

Some researchers believe that symptoms of CFS can be brought on by a triggering event such as surgery.

Searching for a multilayered cause to a disease is even more difficult than trying to identify one causative agent, but research is ongoing to uncover any and every important element in what causes patients to become sick with CFS. That may well be the CFS sufferer's best hope, because as long as the question of cause remains unanswered, the approach to treatment will continue to be equally challenging.

Chapter 5

Treatment

A DIAGNOSIS OF chronic fatigue syndrome (CFS) might bring patients initial relief, because the source of their suffering has finally been identified. However, this relief does not last. "All too often a person who has spent years searching for a diagnosis expects that identification of the illness will bring with it, if not a cure, at the very least an effective treatment plan," explain Erica F. Verrillo and Lauren M. Gellman. "Unfortunately, most of us who have had the illness identified for us have also been told that CFIDS has 'no known cause or cure,' a phrase that invariably creates enough hopelessness to offset any relief the diagnosis may have offered."[45]

Forced to Treat Symptoms

Without knowing the cause of CFS, doctors are forced to treat only the symptoms themselves instead of the underlying problem. And there are further obstacles, including the fact that many people with CFS have an abnormal sensitivity to medications, eliminating the possible usage of these drugs for certain patients. "There is no magic bullet," Katrina Berne warns, "no one universally successful treatment."[46] Patients also tend to vary in terms of their responses to different treatments; a treatment might prove effective for some people but not for others, leaving the doctors having to play a game of trial and error with each new patient. Sometimes this varying response can even occur within one person, where a treatment works at one point but then simply stops working. Also, since different treatments are often attempted at once, it can be difficult to ascertain which one is producing the easing of symptoms. Or the treatment itself can have side effects that actually resemble the symptoms of CFS, making it that much harder to understand exactly what is going on.

But these obstacles have not stopped doctors and researchers from their ongoing efforts to develop treatments that help as many people as possible. Ironically, the way to accomplish this is for doctors to create an individualized treatment plan for each patient in response to that individual's most persistent and debilitating symptoms.

Medication

Since CFS patients have trouble achieving restorative deep sleep, one class of medications commonly prescribed is hypnotics, or sleeping pills, as they are more widely known. These can vary in strength, and doctors begin with the mildest formulas possible, increasing potency as necessary to achieve results. Doctors may also

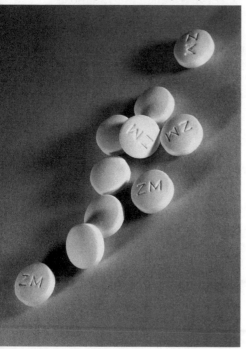

Sleeping pills are commonly prescribed for CFS patients who have trouble achieving restorative deep sleep.

prescribe certain antidepressant drugs, particularly the class known as tricyclics, which not only help the patient sleep, but can also relieve the depression that can accompany CFS and the physical pain that many patients experience. Doctors also occasionally treat pain with low doses of narcotics. A patient taking any of these medications must be closely monitored by a doctor, since the drugs can have side effects that range from mildly inconvenient to life threatening. Also, certain medications—especially the stronger hypnotic drugs and narcotic painkillers—can be addictive, another danger that doctors and patients together must be vigilant to avoid.

Beyond using medications to treat the most obvious or disruptive symptoms, physicians prescribe other drugs to combat any organic abnormalities, such as hormone or immune system deficiencies, found in blood work and other laboratory tests. While doctors are unable to establish a causal relationship between such abnormalities and the symptoms a CFS patient experiences, it is always helpful and important to treat any abnormality that can be identified, such as using synthetic hormone injections to boost hormone levels or prescribing drugs such as gamma globulin and kutapressin to regulate the immune system and jump-start it to work properly. Sometimes these treatments are remarkably effective. Beth, who first became ill with CFS at age thirteen, was able to attend college after repeated intravenous infusions of gamma globulin.

Other drugs may be administered to suppress any active viral infection that seems present, based on highly specific lab tests doctors have developed to track certain viruses. Viral infections cannot be cured the way bacterial infections can be, with antibiotics; however, researchers have developed drugs called antivirals that lower what is called the "viral load," meaning the amount the virus has replicated itself within the system, and force the virus into prolonged latency. These medications have shown varying effectiveness, helping some patients but not all.

Exploring Other Avenues

There are numerous possible drugs that can be helpful to someone with CFS, but medication is not always the only answer. Furthermore, the accompanying risks and side effects of medications must always be considered. Thus, physicians are exploring other avenues of offering relief to CFS patients, both in conjunction with a medication regime and also on their own.

One alternative to medication is vitamin supplements. Because vitamins help regulate cell metabolism, some doctors believe they have the potential to increase energy levels in CFS patients. While doctors emphasize that CFS is not itself a result of a vitamin deficiency, they say that a large enough dose of certain vitamins can boost certain physiological functions. For

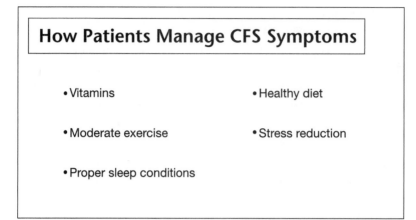

How Patients Manage CFS Symptoms

- Vitamins
- Healthy diet
- Moderate exercise
- Stress reduction
- Proper sleep conditions

instance, Dr. David S. Bell explains that "there is no B12 deficiency state present in CFIDS. . . . [T]he doses that are talked about in CFIDS are not those for vitamin replacement; they are the doses used for a drug effect."[47] B12, along with other B vitamins, are helpful in providing energy, which is why Bell has seen some improvement in the patients given B12 injections. Other vitamins and minerals have shown promise in CFS patients, including vitamin C, calcium, iron, and magnesium. Ongoing studies are attempting to further define exactly which vitamins could be significantly beneficial.

The boost that vitamin supplements provide for a patient's energy reserves are important, since having the energy to exercise regularly can prevent the physical deconditioning that often accompanies CFS. The benefits of a well-designed exercise program for a CFS patient are extensive; along with keeping the body well conditioned, exercise also increases blood circulation and improves cardiac fitness, reduces stress and depression by elevating levels of mood-lifting chemicals (endorphins) in the body, and even increases the body's pain threshold, easing the aches and pains that are common in people with CFS.

Doctors do not advise their patients to force themselves to exercise when the action is excruciating. However, over time they do recommend that patients slowly build moderate exercise into their routines. They remind their patients not to push themselves or attempt any rigorous workouts. Instead, they suggest patients start with low-impact workouts such as walking or swimming, and also basic stretching and yoga. Some patients, after experiencing a degree of improvement, are able to move on to more vigorous exercise over time.

Because CFS patients generally report disturbed sleep patterns or complain that sleep does not leave them feeling rested, proper sleep hygiene is especially key for someone with CFS. Sleep hygiene involves taking certain steps to make one's environment conducive to sleep, such as keeping the bedroom dark and at a moderate temperature, and avoiding using the room for any stressful nonsleep activities, such as work, so that the room is associated only with sleep. Practicing good sleep hygiene also means avoiding the consumption of anything that promotes wakefulness, such as caffeine, past midafternoon and any liquids after early evening. Sticking to roughly the same bedtime and wake-up time every day, taking some time to relax before bedtime, and avoiding naps if they tend to disrupt nighttime sleep are all recommendations for good sleep hygiene.

Doctors often advise their CFS patients to engage in moderate amounts of low-impact exercise such as swimming.

Since the fatigue that accompanies CFS is much more severe than a healthy person's fatigue, sleep hygiene alone cannot provide the restoration needed. However, it is a treatment option that can offer at least some help to certain patients, and people with CFS are usually eager to combine as many treatments as necessary in order to feel better.

Since depression is so closely associated with CFS, many doctors advise their patients to seek counseling. They also emphasize the importance of a support network to minimize the patient's sense of isolation and alienation. This can take the form of family and friends who understand the limitations forced on the patient and help accommodate the individual, and also networks of people who have CFS and stay in touch to help one another both emotionally and by offering concrete advice on coping with the everyday challenges posed by the disease.

An Alternative Approach

Still, all these approaches to dealing with their condition often fail to bring relief, and desperate CFS patients who feel that the mainstream medical community has failed them often seek help from what is known as alternative medicine. Treatments considered alternative are not officially recognized by regulatory agencies like the Food and Drug Administration, taught in medical schools, or scientifically proven safe and effective.

Alternative medicine, also called complementary medicine, is a very broad term, encompassing many different theories and practices. In general, however, treatments fitting under this heading involve a focus on the whole patient along with the patient's lifestyle and environment, instead of just on the patient's symptoms. Whereas a mainstream physician, for instance, would concentrate on finding a biological explanation and corresponding treatment for a CFS patient's fatigue or headaches, an alternative medicine practitioner would look at these symptoms in the broader context of every aspect of the patient's physical, emotional, and spiritual well-being.

The line, however, between "alternative" and "traditional" medicine has been growing increasingly blurry as more and more mainstream doctors prescribe alternative treatments for patients after seeing evidence of their effectiveness. This is especially the case with a disease like CFS where doctors are often as frustrated as patients are by the ineffectiveness of medical intervention to relieve symptoms. Thus, there is an ever-growing range of alternative treatments for CFS, with some gaining more popularity and acceptance than others.

Changes in Lifestyle

One treatment recommended by the alternative medical community involves a drastic change in diet. Not only do alternative practitioners suggest increasing the consumption of nutritious foods such as fruits, vegetables, and whole grains, but many also emphasize the potential ill effects of consuming substances such as sugar, white flour, caffeine, and alcohol on the system of someone with CFS. "I am constantly astonished at the number of people who complain about being tired who drink more than ten cups of coffee a day," Dr. Jacob Teitelbaum remarks. "Caffeine is a loan shark for energy."[48] While caffeine may provide an initial energy boost to a CFS patient, after the effects wear off, the patient experiences a severe plummeting of energy, leaving the patient feeling even more exhausted than before. Teitelbaum and others also warn CFS patients to be tested for unknown food allergies, since these, they contend, can cause or contribute to many of the CFS symptoms. While most mainstream doctors do not view diet modification as a strong treatment on its own, they tend to acknowledge that a healthier diet would in any case be beneficial. Bell, somewhat skeptical of the strict diets that preach a total avoidance of substances such as white flour or sugar, claims that he has never seen a consistent response in patients trying various special CFS diets. However, he notes that "good nutrition . . . make[s] sense whenever a person is ill, whether with CFIDS or any other disease."[49]

Some practitioners of alternative medicine advise CFS patients to drastically increase their consumption of fruits, vegetables, and whole grains.

Along with a change in diet, practitioners of alternative medicine also recommend efforts to reduce stress—and this is one lifestyle change agreed on by all experts who have treated CFS patients. As Verrillo and Gellman explain:

> Difficulty coping with stressful situations may arise as one of the earliest symptoms of CFIDS. . . . Many people with CFIDS remark that a stressful job or home environment during the early stages of the illness contributed to the severity of the illness at onset; patients in the recovery phase often note that emotional stress can bring on relapse; and those who are severely ill experience profound exacerbation [worsening] of symptoms when placed in stressful situations or environments.[50]

They are quick to point out that this does not prove that CFS is caused or induced by stress (something that some people still believe), but rather that "stress can prolong, or worsen, the disease process."[51]

While the exact role stress plays in CFS may remain in debate, the link between stress and a worsening of symptoms is clear. Thus, stress reduction is viewed as a key element to any CFS treatment plan, sometimes meaning that a person must make radical changes in the work, home, personal, and social spheres. "Patients with CFIDS must make profound adjustments in the way they see themselves in the world and modify the way they live accordingly,"[52] insist Verrillo and Gellman.

Other Options

The world of alternative medicine extends far beyond lifestyle changes, and many of the more controversial alternative therapies that have been used to treat CFS include herbs, homeopathy, osteopathy, chiropractic, acupuncture, and acupressure.

"Herbal medicine can be of great assistance in the treatment of chronic fatigue syndrome," Burton Goldberg argues. "Each herb has one or more specific healing property, an advantage enabling the skilled herbalist to design a treatment program targeting specific ailments or imbalances."[53] Just as various medications are aimed at boosting the immune system, increasing energy, or im-

Some experts contend that herbal medications like ginkgo biloba are helpful in treating CFS.

proving other bodily functions, there are herbs that purportedly aid in these capacities as well. For instance, there are herbs thought to increase cognitive function, to reduce fatigue, and even supposedly to help boost the function of the adrenal glands. The mainstream medical community's position on herbal remedies is that as long as the herbs the patient plans to use are widely considered safe, including them in the treatment plan can sometimes be helpful.

Doctors are typically more skeptical of the effectiveness of homeopathy, an approach to treatment that is based on the idea that a substance that *causes* specific symptoms can, in highly diluted concentrations, stimulate the body's natural ability to overcome symptoms. "Most mainstream medical practitioners regard the practice of homeopathy with suspicion," Berne relates, "and the American Medical Association (AMA) has taken an exclusionary view of homeopathy, which lacks governmental licensing or regulation."[54] Some patients who have tried homeopathic treatments, which can be expensive and usually are not covered by health insurance, have reported a decrease in symptoms, while others have not.

Chiropractors and osteopaths have also had some success treating CFS symptoms, particularly the physical pain that is commonly reported by CFS patients. Both professions focus on physically manipulating the skeletal system, in the belief that misalignment of the spine causes symptoms such as headache, stomach problems, and generalized pain in the body and muscles. Chiropractic adjustments focus on the spine, back, and neck, while osteopathic adjustments may involve other parts of the body as well.

A chiropractor adjusts a youngster's neck. Some chiropractors have had success treating some CFS symptoms.

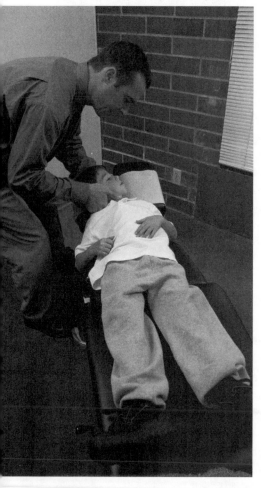

Acupuncture and acupressure, treatments derived from Chinese medicine, directly address the issue of attaining balance in the body. In acupuncture, small needles are inserted at various so-called energy points on the body that are supposed to be key to overall well-being. These same energy points are addressed by acupressure, except that instead of inserting needles into them, the practitioner applies external pressure. Again, some patients have found a limited amount of relief from these treatments.

Treating Children

While adults have a vast number of treatment options available from both the traditional and alternative medical worlds, children are not given quite the same choices. Because young people's bodies and minds are still developing, doctors are reluctant to prescribe some of the medications they would use for adult patients. However, studies have shown that some regimens, such as vitamins, herbs considered safe, and over-the-counter pain relievers and antihistamines, can help children and adolescents cope with pain and achieve better sleep. As with adults, a reasonable amount of exercise is advised, along with a focus on balanced nutrition, and parents are also encouraged to help their children modify their lifestyles to accommodate the symptoms.

Psychologists have developed techniques to help children cope with the potential cognitive difficulties of CFS and remain active in school, and parents can work with their children and with teachers to ensure that the learning process is able to continue. Since children with CFS often lose their ability to concentrate for long periods of time, many of the techniques are geared toward reducing the child's anxiety, cutting down on any distractions such as background noise, and conveying the material in shorter, more digestible amounts rather than trying to load the child down with too much information at once. Frequent study breaks and adequate rest are highly recommended, as is establishing a regular schedule and keeping to it as much as possible.

The Big Picture

The diagnosis of CFS can initially be overwhelming because there is no known cure. However, there is a multitude of treatment options available, and patients of all ages and overall states of health often find some treatment or combination of treatments that can offer a certain degree of relief. Unfortunately, people with CFS often must expend what little time and energy they have continually exploring new ways to manage their illness. Meanwhile, researchers remain devoted to developing new and more effective treatments, some of which are already showing promise.

Chapter 6

Looking Forward

W HILE MUCH HAS been learned about chronic fatigue syndrome (CFS) over the past few decades, definitive clues regarding a cause or a cure for the disease still elude researchers. However, there is growing hope that this will change as more time and resources are devoted to CFS.

Living with CFS

The disease that was once dismissed as an affliction for self-indulgent "yuppies" has been taken more seriously in recent years as people realize just how widespread and potentially debilitating CFS is. Yet, with no cure in sight, CFS sufferers and those around them can find some reassurance from prominent individuals whose accomplishments are living proof that for many, it *is* possible to function to some extent in spite of the disease.

Author Laura Hillenbrand, who has CFS, has had numerous interviews about the success of her *New York Times* best-selling book *Seabiscuit: An American Legend*. In a number of published interviews, Hillenbrand talked freely about her battle with CFS, noting that while she was able to write an entire book, she had to write every word from her bedroom because she was too weak to move much farther.

People with CFS are quick to emphasize, as Hillenbrand does, the balance between struggling not to let CFS prevent one from pursuing goals, and acknowledging and accepting the very real limitations that the disease can place on this pursuit. Olympic Gold Medal–winning women's soccer star Michelle Akers discussed this balance when she made her CFS diagnosis public in congressional testimony about the drastic nature of the disease in an effort to persuade lawmakers to increase funding for research. And in an open and personal essay, Akers describes in detail what she managed to do while sick, and what every exertion on the field would cost her.

> At my best, I could play 15–20 (or if really lucky 30) minutes of a 90 minute match, train in light to moderate intensity to stay in some kind of shape for National Team, and maintain a skeletal appearance schedule for my sponsor, Umbro. The repercussions of those activities [were] migraines and overwhelming fatigue during and especially after [the exertion] for days or weeks. It was a constant "tradeout." The trade being the ability to maintain my contact and involvement in the "normal" world and my career . . . with the devastating effects of that involvement on my body.[55]

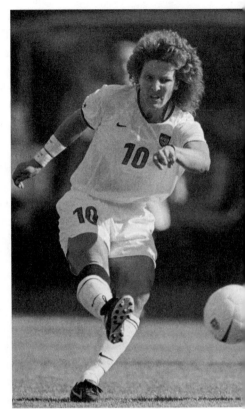

Michelle Akers of the U.S. Women's national soccer team was forced by CFS to retire from her sport.

Akers—once called the greatest women's soccer player ever—was forced to retire from soccer just shy of the 2000 Olympics because of the incredible toll CFS took on her body, proving the point often made by CFS sufferers that sheer force of will is not enough to combat the effects of this disease.

Those who speak out about CFS are at pains to emphasize that theirs is a real illness that needs to be taken seriously. Another Olympic athlete to speak publicly is Amy Peterson, who was chosen by her Olympic teammates to carry the American flag at the opening ceremony of the 2002 Olympics. It was Peterson's fifth time competing as a speed skater in the winter Olympic Games, a feat made particularly impressive in light of the CFS diagnosis she received in 1997. Peterson, like Akers, made an effort to use her time in the spotlight to discuss the horror and reality of CFS. In an interview on NBC's *Today* she shared her frustration with having to respond to people who would hear of her illness and assume she just "gets tired," like everyone else. "There's definitely a difference [between being tired and having CFS],"[56] Peterson stated emphatically in the interview.

Meanwhile, along with the celebrities speaking up about CFS, support group leaders have petitioned the federal government for increased funding for research into the cause of CFS while conducting their own fund-raising as well. More and more individuals and support groups have pooled their resources and efforts to spread the word about CFS, culminating on May 12, the designated Awareness Day for CFS and fibromyalgia since 1992. As more medical journals carry articles on CFS, mass-market magazines and newspapers have increased their own coverage. Many women's magazines—probably due to the fact that more women than men are affected by CFS—now note the existence of Awareness Day in their May issues.

Despite suffering from CFS, American speed skater Amy Peterson competes in the 500 meter short track event during the 2002 Olympics.

The increased publicity for CFS, combined with calls for action from the ever-growing numbers of people being diagnosed with CFS, has led to increased funding for research on the disease. With more money available, scientists are eagerly pursuing a deeper understanding of CFS, and several studies seem to hold the potential to yield important insights.

New Research into the Cause

The most persistent and challenging mystery of CFS remains its cause. Researchers continue to investigate the possible role of the immune system, the endocrine system, and various viruses in causing CFS. Meanwhile, doctors have found evidence pointing in the direction of several new possibilities. Researchers at the University of Washington's Chronic Fatigue Syndrome Cooperative Research Center are currently investigating the role of genetics in determining susceptibility to CFS and fibromyalgia. One study focuses on sets of twins in which one or both individuals have one of these illnesses. The purpose of the study is to attain a clearer distinction between which risk factors are inherited and which are environmental, something that can be accomplished much more easily with subjects who have similar or identical genetic material. "Say you study two people with the same genetic material," explains center researcher and associate director Dr. Niloofar Afari. "If one of them has a disease or shows certain test results and the other one does not, you can figure there may be environmental factors at play." And, of course, the reverse is true as well. "If [the twins] do show a difference, you can attribute that to what's different about the twins, which is their environment," Afari reiterates. "If they don't show a difference, you can attribute that to what's the same—their genetics."[57] The university is studying both identical and fraternal twins. Identical twins share all of the same genetic material, making them ideal subjects for the study. Fraternal twins usually share about half of their genetic material, which is still enough to provide clues as to whether one might inherit a susceptibility to CFS and to help researchers study what factors could cause only one person in the pair to develop the disease, even when both appear genetically susceptible.

Identical twins pose for a photograph. New studies of twins are aimed at identifying environmental causes of CFS.

The research is ongoing, but preliminary findings are promising. One early result that researchers found intriguing was that sets of twins labeled "discordant," meaning that one twin was sick with CFS or fibromyalgia and the other was not, actually showed similar abnormal results on certain lab tests. "For example," Afari explains, "in exercise testing, [the twins] both appear to be doing similarly—but similarly poorly." Yet only one of these twins is actually exhibiting the full set of symptoms for CFS or fibromyalgia, leading the researchers to wonder why the other is not. "One of the things we're focusing on is perception," Afari notes.

> Two people could have exactly the same experience, yet the body systems of one would sense it, perceive it, differently than those of the other person. . . . It doesn't mean that you think you have CFS and therefore you do. It means that the bodies of people with CFS may sense things differently. . . . There's no doubt that people feel pain. You give them a strong enough stimulus, they're going to say "ouch." But at what point does somebody say "ouch"? That's perception.[58]

Afari believes that further research into this question could lead to possible diagnostic markers for CFS and perhaps also to forms of treatment or even a method of preventing CFS or fibromyalgia from occurring in someone with a genetic predisposition.

Another possible causal factor that has received a great deal of attention from researchers in recent years is orthostatic intolerance (OI). OI is defined as the development of symptoms while standing or sitting upright. The number of CFS patients confined to bed led researchers to explore the significance of this problem, and in 1995 Dr. Peter Rowe first published a study showing evidence of one form of OI in people with CFS. Rowe found that 96 percent of the CFS patients in his study experienced a sharp drop in systolic blood pressure when they stood up from a reclining position. The drop in blood pressure was accompanied by an intensifying of other CFS symptoms as well, such as pain and fatigue.

Since then, Dr. Julian Stewart, among others, has explored the role of another form of OI called postural orthostatic tachycardia syndrome (POTS), also known as chronic orthostatic intolerance. In POTS, a person experiences a rapid increase in heart rate during the first ten minutes of standing. Stewart, a pediatric cardiologist, says that "the children [diagnosed with CFS] I've seen have almost all had POTS."[59] POTS has also been found in a significant number of adult CFS patients. Symptoms of POTS resemble many of the common CFS symptoms, such as lightheadedness, dizziness, nausea, fatigue, headache, and vision problems.

OI, researchers already know, is primarily a problem of the autonomic nervous system, the part of the nervous system that controls involuntary functions such as heartbeat and breathing. Thus, the connection established between POTS and CFS may lend credence to the theory that CFS is caused by a malfunction of the autonomic nervous system. However, there is still no actual cause-effect relationship identified between POTS and CFS; the existence of a relationship on its own cannot determine which problem causes the other. Researchers such as Stewart and Rowe continue to investigate this relationship, however, hoping that one day their studies will yield a more conclusive answer.

Implications for Treatment

Since treatments already exist for OI, studies have been done to explore the effectiveness of these treatments for people diagnosed with CFS. Stewart has seen a number of his CFS patients improve after receiving standard POTS treatments, including increased water and salt consumption and certain medications that treat low blood volume and cause blood vessels to constrict.

Some researchers have expanded the investigation into OI and looked at the possibility that it is actually not just low circulating blood volume, but in particular a reduced amount of red blood cell mass that is causing the CFS symptoms. Addressing the possibility that low red blood cell mass is the problem, researchers at the University of Miami are conducting a study with the drug Procrit. "In chronic fatigue [syndrome] about 60 to 70 percent of the individuals we found have a deficit in red

Red blood cells travel through an artery. Reduced red blood cell mass may cause one form of orthostatic intolerance, which some researchers believe is somehow linked to CFS.

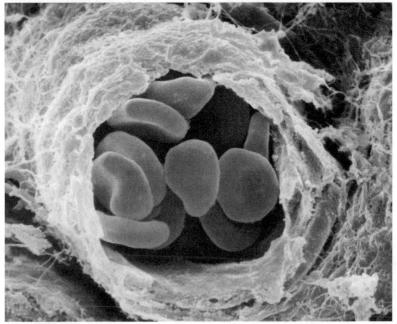

blood cell production and it's not picked up by normal medical tests,"[60] Dr. Barry Hurwitz revealed in a television interview about the study. Procrit is typically used to treat anemia in cancer patients, but researchers hope that since the drug helps boost red blood cell production, it might help alleviate CFS symptoms. While the study is ongoing, one participant was already enthusiastic about her own response to the treatments. "We had a party at our house for the first time in about four years," Jean Gaudreau shared in the same television segment. "I felt that good. We had a Christmas tree for the first time in a number of years. I was able to clean the house. I was able to do functions. I could work. I was able to work a 40-hour week. It was just amazing the changes."[61]

While these treatments show promise, they are not universally effective, nor are the suggested causes they are treating (OI and low red blood cell mass) proven to cause symptoms in all CFS patients. Therefore, many efforts are still being made to increase the effectiveness of other treatments for CFS that are already in use. One treatment in particular that has gained acceptance from doctors is cognitive behavior therapy (CBT).

CBT involves working with patients to modify the way they view themselves and their illness, in order to help them adopt appropriate coping mechanisms. "[CBT] does not deny the biological basis of illness," emphasizes behavioral specialist Dr. Michael Sharpe. "[It] assumes that psychological (cognitive, behavioral and emotional) and social aspects of illness are interrelated, so that a change in one can produce change in others."[62] In other words, even if a person is truly sick, it is still possible that a change in focus and thinking patterns can lessen the severity with which the patient *experiences* the symptoms. Sharpe adds:

> Thoughts a person has when they're depressed, negative thoughts about their future, are not just consequences of a biological process, but also factors that keep [the biological process] going. There is actually some evidence from several studies that patients who have an exclusive, strong prediction that they have a physical disease have a worse prognosis than those who don't. The patients may be right: maybe they actually know more than

their physicians about [CFS]. But it also raises the possibility that the things that go with that belief, such as loss of control and helplessness, may actually perpetuate [the illness].[63]

Of course, the idea that one's attitude affects the course of an illness is not true just for CFS, but for many diseases and disorders. Positive thinking and a hopeful outlook have been proven repeatedly to increase a sick person's chances for recovery. However, since CFS can reach into so many corners of a patient's life, it can be particularly important for people with CFS fatigue to maintain as positive an attitude as possible.

Like the many other treatments used for CFS patients, CBT has been effective in some cases, but is still not a cure, nor does it work for everyone. People with CFS continue to experiment with combinations of old and new treatments, looking to experience as much relief from their symptoms as possible until a cure is identified.

Prospects for Recovery

The need to find a cure is compelling. According to the Centers for Disease Control and Prevention, only about 12 percent of people diagnosed with CFS experience a full and complete recovery, meaning that they return to their previously healthy states. However, many CFS patients improve significantly following their initial or worst periods of sickness. "In our experience," says Dr. Anthony Komaroff, an expert on CFS, "approximately ten to fifteen percent of patients have fully recovered from CFS. [But] the vast majority of patients feel sickest in the first six to twelve months and improve to some degree over the course of time."[64] One patient who has suffered for thirteen years says that he never felt any real relief from any of the many treatments his doctors tried. Yet, over time, his most severe symptoms eased, allowing him to leave the house and to think more clearly.

Patients and physicians also point out that it can be difficult to differentiate between having actually recovered from symptoms and having learned to cope with them better. People with CFS learn to accept a continuum of sickness and wellness, rather than

A CFS patient works with a therapist in an effort to build mastery of the disease.

a more rigidly defined contrast of "sick" and "well." Patients experience better and worse days, and sometimes better and worse *years.* Treatment manuals discuss periods of remission, when symptoms ease dramatically or even completely, along with the possibility of relapses, and most CFS patients describe having numerous ups and downs over the course of their illness. For example, one young CFS patient notes that with treatment she was able to leave the bed where she had been confined for years and attend college, yet that same patient cites a three-week period of time in which she pushed herself too hard and ended up back in bed for another three years.

While such cycles of health and illness appear to be the norm for adults, prospects for a more complete recovery in children seem to be slightly better. A follow-up study of some of the young patients Dr. David S. Bell saw during the Lyndonville outbreak in the 1980s revealed that 80 percent of the children had either fully recovered or shown some improvement. However, Bell cautions that some of the patients claiming to have improved have simply adapted their lifestyles to their symptoms, not actually achieved a lessening of symptoms. Moreover, the remaining 20 percent of survey respondents were still disabled by the disease.

There is no way to predict a patient's chances for improvement, but Bell has observed factors that appear to be significant. In his follow-up of the Lyndonville children, Bell found that those children who missed the least amount of school and showed some improvement during the early years of their illness were more likely to experience recovery, possibly indicating that children who experience the most severe symptoms at onset of illness and during the early years are less likely to improve than those whose symptoms start off less severe and worsen gradually. In both adults and children, the development of more severe neurological symptoms seems to reduce the chances for improvement.

While CFS offers few of its victims hope for a full recovery, most patients do experience some degree of improvement, and new treatments are being tested all the time. Meanwhile, researchers continue to search for answers to the many questions that still surround this puzzling disease, in the hopes that one day patients' suffering will be put to an end once and for all.

Notes

Introduction: Chronic Fatigue Syndrome—
More than Just Being Tired

1. Quoted in Katrina Berne, *Chronic Fatigue Syndrome, Fibromyalgia and Other Invisible Illnesses: The Comprehensive Guide.* Alameda, CA: Hunter House, Inc., 2002, p. 24.
2. Hillary Johnson, *Osler's Web: Inside the Labyrinth of the Chronic Fatigue Syndrome Epidemic.* New York: Penguin Books, 1996, p. 219.

Chapter 1: A Mystery Disease

3. George M. Beard, *American Nervousness: Its Causes and Consequences, a Supplement to Nervous Exhaustion (Neurasthenia).* New York: G.P. Putnam, 1881, p. 96.
4. Hillary Johnson, "Journey into Fear: The Growing Nightmare of Epstein-Barr Virus," *Rolling Stone,* July 16–30, 1987, p. 58.
5. Quoted in Geoffrey Cowley with Mary Hager and Nadine Joseph, "Chronic Fatigue Syndrome: A Modern Medical Mystery," *Newsweek,* November 12, 1990, p. 64.
6. Quoted in Cowley, "Chronic Fatigue Syndrome," p. 62.
7. Ron Winslow, "CDC to Study Illness Derided As 'Yuppie Flu,'" *Wall Street Journal,* November 19, 1990.
8. Berne, *Chronic Fatigue Syndrome,* pp. 11–12.
9. Quoted in Johnson, "Journey into Fear," p. 141.

Chapter 2: Symptoms and Diagnosis

10. David S. Bell, *The Doctor's Guide to Chronic Fatigue Syndrome: Understanding, Treating, and Living with CFIDS.* Cambridge, MA: Perseus Books, 1995, p. 25.
11. Erica F. Verrillo and Lauren M. Gellman, *Chronic Fatigue Syndrome: A Treatment Guide.* New York: St. Martin's Press, 1997, p. 21.

12. Berne, *Chronic Fatigue Syndrome*, pp. 11–12.
13. Greg Charles Fisher, *Chronic Fatigue Syndrome: A Comprehensive Guide to Symptoms, Treatments, and Solving the Practical Problems of CFS*. New York: Warner Books, 1997, p. 20.
14. Johnson, "Journey into Fear," p. 59.
15. Johnson, "Journey into Fear," p. 59.
16. Beth, interview by author, New Jersey, May 17, 2002.
17. Bell, *Doctor's Guide to Chronic Fatigue Syndrome*, pp. 72–73.
18. Bell, *Doctor's Guide to Chronic Fatigue Syndrome*, p. 73.
19. Berne, *Chronic Fatigue Syndrome*, p. 83.
20. Bell, *Doctor's Guide to Chronic Fatigue Syndrome*, p. 25.
21. Bell, *Doctor's Guide to Chronic Fatigue Syndrome*, p. 73.
22. Verrillo and Gellman, *Chronic Fatigue Syndrome*, p. 327.

Chapter 3: Problems and Complications

23. Verrillo and Gellman, *Chronic Fatigue Syndrome*, p. 54.
24. Johnson, "Journey into Fear," p. 58.
25. John, interview by author, New Jersey, May 24, 2002.
26. Bell, *Doctor's Guide to Chronic Fatigue Syndrome*, p. 45.
27. Bell, *Doctor's Guide to Chronic Fatigue Syndrome*, p. 61.
28. Berne, *Chronic Fatigue Syndrome*, p. 49.
29. Bell, *Doctor's Guide to Chronic Fatigue Syndrome*, p. 54.
30. Johnson, "Journey into Fear," p. 59.
31. Fisher, *Chronic Fatigue Syndrome*, p. 120.
32. John, interview.
33. Jon Sterling, interview by author, New Jersey, June 3, 2002.
34. Beth, interview.

Chapter 4: The Question of a Cause

35. Berne, *Chronic Fatigue Syndrome*, p. 146.
36. Jacob Teitelbaum, *From Fatigued to Fantastic! A Guide to Overcoming Severe Chronic Fatigue, Poor Sleep, Achiness, "Brain Fog," Increased Thirst, Bowel Disorders, Recurrent Infections, and Exhaustion*. New York: Penguin Putnam, 2001, p. 59.
37. Bell, *Doctor's Guide to Chronic Fatigue Syndrome*, p. 95.
38. Berne, *Chronic Fatigue Syndrome*, p. 149.
39. Verrillo and Gellman, *Chronic Fatigue Syndrome*, p. 291.
40. Burton Goldberg and the editors of *Alternative Medicine*

Digest, Alternative Medicine Guide to Chronic Fatigue, Fibromyalgia and Environmental Illness. Tiburon, CA: Future Medicine Publishing, 1998, p. 164.

41. Verrillo and Gellman, *Chronic Fatigue Syndrome*, p. 291.
42. John, interview.
43. Bell, *Doctor's Guide to Chronic Fatigue Syndrome*, p. 3l.
44. Berne, *Chronic Fatigue Syndrome*, pp. 113–14.

Chapter 5: Treatment
45. Verrillo and Gellman, *Chronic Fatigue Syndrome*, p. 1.
46. Berne, *Chronic Fatigue Syndrome*, p. 210.
47. Bell, *Doctor's Guide to Chronic Fatigue Syndrome*, p. 176.
48. Teitelbaum, *From Fatigued to Fantastic!* p. 15.
49. Bell, *Doctor's Guide to Chronic Fatigue Syndrome*, p. 154.
50. Verrillo and Gellman, *Chronic Fatigue Syndrome*, pp. 287–88.
51. Verrillo and Gellman, *Chronic Fatigue Syndrome*, pp. 287–88.
52. Verrillo and Gellman, *Chronic Fatigue Syndrome*, p. 284.
53. Goldberg, *Alternative Medicine Guide*, p. 318.
54. Berne, *Chronic Fatigue Syndrome*, p. 200.

Chapter 6: Looking Forward
55. Michelle Akers, "My History with CFIDS," Soccer Outreach International. www.socceroutreach.com.
56. Amy Peterson, interview by Jamie Gangel, Today NBC, February 8, 2002.
57. Niloofar Afari, interview by *CFIDS Chronicle*. www.cfids.org.
58. Afari, interview.
59. Julian Stewart, interview by author, New Jersey, May 22, 2002.
60. Barry Hurwitz, interview by Ian Smith, "Drug Could Help Chronic Fatigue: Syndrome Linked to Red Blood Cell Production," WNBC, May 15, 2002. www.wnbc.com.
61. Jean Gaudreau, interview by Ian Smith, "Drug Could Help Chronic Fatigue: Syndrome Linked to Red Blood Cell Production," WNBC, May 15, 2002. www.wnbc.com.
62. Quoted in Vicki L. Carpman, "Cognitive Behavioral Therapy: Implications for CFS," *CFIDS Chronicle*. www.cfids.org.
63. Quoted in Carpman, "Cognitive Behavioral Therapy."
64. Quoted in Fisher, *Chronic Fatigue Syndrome*, p. 165.

Glossary

allergy: An overreaction of the immune system to a normally harmless substance.

antibody: Something that the body creates in response to a foreign invader such as a bacterium, virus, or parasite.

autoimmune disease: A disease that results from the immune system becoming confused and attacking the body's own cells and tissues.

autonomic nervous system: The division of the nervous system that regulates involuntary actions, such as digestion and response to stress.

blood pressure: The force of blood inside blood vessels.

cognitive: Related to mental processes, including awareness, perception, reasoning, and judgment.

contagious: Transmissible by direct or indirect contact.

debilitating: Causing severe decrease in the ability to function.

depression: A psychiatric disorder that causes great sadness and affects a person's appetite, sleep patterns, energy levels, and desire to engage in activities that were once pleasurable.

endocrine system: The set of glands, for example, the pituitary, responsible for secreting hormones.

environmental factor: Something that is external and not related to one's genetic makeup.

epidemic: A rapidly spreading infection affecting many individuals in an area or a population at the same time.

fibromyalgia: A condition with a long list of symptoms, some of which closely resemble those of chronic fatigue syndrome, including widespread aching, stiffness, and fatigue. The condition is defined by the presence of specific body tender points.

genetic trait: Any characteristic that is determined by the DNA contained within one's cells.

hormones: Chemical messengers made by the body's endocrine glands that regulate different bodily functions, including mood, growth, energy, and appetite.

hypochondriac: A patient with imaginary symptoms and ailments.

immune system: The aggregate of organs, tissues, cells, and cell products that protects the body and defends against invaders.

lymph nodes: Small masses of tissue responsible for filtering bacteria and foreign particles from the lymphatic fluid.

malaise: A vague feeling of physical and emotional discomfort.

migraine: A severe headache that is often accompanied by nausea and sensitivity to light and sound.

natural killer cells: Specialized blood cells that are the first line of defense against viruses and other invaders to the body.

neurology: The medical branch that deals with the nervous system and disorders affecting it.

onset: The beginning or early stages of an illness.

opportunistic infection: An infection that normally does not cause disease, except when the body's immune system is impaired.

organic cause: A cause that is physical rather than psychological.

poliomyelitis (polio): A highly infectious viral disease that causes inflammation in the spinal cord and brain stem, leading to paralysis, muscular atrophy, and often permanent disability.

psychiatry: The branch of medicine that deals with the diagnosis, treatment, and prevention of mental and emotional disorders.

psychosomatic: Having physical symptoms that originate from mental or emotional causes.

red blood cells: The cells responsible for carrying oxygen to the rest of the cells in the body.

relapse: A return to a previous level of sickness after having experienced an improvement.

remission: A period of recovery from symptoms of illness.

rheumatologist: A physician specializing in rheumatic diseases, which can involve the muscles, tendons, joints, bones, or nerves.

Organizations to Contact

American Association for Chronic Fatigue Syndrome (AACFS)
c/o Harborview Medical Center
PO Box 359780
Seattle, WA 98104
(206) 521-1932
website: www.aacfs.org

AACFS collects information from different health care professionals and provides the latest news and research results.

CFIDS Association of America, Inc.
PO Box 220398
Charlotte, NC 28222-0398
(800) 442-3437
Resource line: (704) 365-2343
website: www.cfids.org

This national organization provides information and resources to people with chronic fatigue syndrome, and also strives to protect their rights and needs through various lobbying efforts. It publishes a quarterly journal, *CFIDS Chronicle*, full of articles on the latest research as well as personal stories and coping advice. It also coordinates support groups across the country.

CFIDS in Youth
website: www.cfids.org
E-mail: youth@cfids.org

A subdivision of the CFIDS Association of America, this part of the organization concentrates on offering information and support for young people with chronic fatigue syndrome.

National CFIDS Foundation
103 Aletha Rd.
Needham, MA 02492
(781) 449-3535
website: www.ncf-net.org

This organization focuses on raising funds for research into chronic fatigue syndrome and publicizing important information about the disease.

For Further Reading

Books

Majid Ali, *The Canary and Chronic Fatigue Syndrome*. Denville, NJ: Lifespan Press, 1994. Explains one theory on the origin of CFS and corresponding advice on treatment.

David S. Bell, Mary Z. Robinson, Jean Pollard, Tom Robinson, and Bonnie Floyd, *A Parents' Guide to CFIDS: How to Be an Advocate for Your Child with Chronic Fatigue Immune Dysfunction Syndrome*. Binghampton, NY: Haworth Press, 1999. A manual for parents with children diagnosed with CFS.

Timothy Kenny, *Living with Chronic Fatigue Syndrome: A Personal Story of the Struggle for Recovery*. New York: Thunder's Mouth Press, 1994. A journalist talks about his personal struggle with CFS.

Susan M. Lark, *Chronic Fatigue Self-Help Book: Effective Solutions for Conditions Associated with CFS, Candida, Allergies, PMS, Menopause, Anemia, Low Thyroid, and Depression*. Berkeley, CA: Celestial Arts, 1993. A self-help guide to treat fatigue. Includes nutrition advice, exercises, meal plans and recipes, suggestions for vitamins, minerals, and herbs.

Websites

About.com: Chronic Fatigue Syndrome/Fibromyalgia (chronic fatigue.about.com). This website offers links to information on every facet of the disease, from symptoms and diagnosis to current research. There are also personal stories from people struggling with CFS.

CFS Information International (www.cfs.inform.dk). This website combines information from across the world on CFS and fibromyalgia.

CFS News (Co-Cure) (www.cfs-news.org). This website contains a great deal of information on CFS, including links to transcripts from a weekly radio show about CFS no longer on the air.

WebMD (www.webmd.com). This general health website contains articles on various aspects of CFS.

Works Consulted

Books

George M. Beard, *American Nervousness: Its Causes and Consequences, a Supplement to Nervous Exhaustion (Neurasthenia)*. New York: G.P. Putnam, 1881. Discusses theories on the nineteenth-century illness Beard identified as "neurasthenia."

David S. Bell, *The Doctor's Guide to Chronic Fatigue Syndrome: Understanding, Treating, and Living with CFIDS*. Cambridge, MA: Perseus Books, 1995. A clear explanation of the medical components and history of CFS, with specific references to his own experiences with young patients in particular.

Katrina Berne, *Chronic Fatigue Syndrome, Fibromyalgia and Other Invisible Illnesses: The Comprehensive Guide*. Alameda, CA: Hunter House, Inc., 2002. A very detailed account of all aspects of CFS, including the numerous possible complications and body systems affected.

Greg Charles Fisher, *Chronic Fatigue Syndrome: A Comprehensive Guide to Symptoms, Treatments, and Solving the Practical Problems of CFS*. New York: Warner Books, 1997. A personal account of Fisher's and his wife's struggles with CFS and the treatments they found helpful.

Burton Goldberg and the editors of *Alternative Medicine Digest, Alternative Medicine Guide to Chronic Fatigue, Fibromyalgia and Environmental Illness*. Tiburon, CA: Future Medicine Publishing, 1998. An in-depth examination of the effectiveness of various alternative treatments on CFS patients, and theories on what causes the illness.

Jay A. Goldstein, *Betrayal by the Brain: The Neurologic Basis of Chronic Fatigue Syndrome, Fibromyalgia Syndrome and Related*

Neural Network Disorders. Binghampton, NY: Haworth Press, 1996. A doctor's exploration of the neurology of CFS, in medical language.

Hillary Johnson, *Osler's Web: Inside the Labyrinth of the Chronic Fatigue Syndrome Epidemic*. New York: Penguin Books, 1996. An overview of the political history of CFS and its classification as a disease.

Mari Skelly and Andrea Helm, *Alternative Treatments for Fibromyalgia and Chronic Fatigue Syndrome*. Alameda, CA: Hunter House, 1999. Provides a wide range of treatment tips described by health practitioners, with firsthand accounts from patients.

Jacob Teitelbaum, *From Fatigued to Fantastic! A Guide to Overcoming Severe Chronic Fatigue, Poor Sleep, Achiness, "Brain Fog," Increased Thirst, Bowel Disorders, Recurrent Infections, and Exhaustion*. New York: Penguin Putnam, 2001. Provides evidence from Teitelbaum's clinical practice on treatments that work for specific, identified abnormalities.

Erica F. Verrillo and Lauren M. Gellman, *Chronic Fatigue Syndrome: A Treatment Guide*. New York: St. Martin's Press, 1997. An overview of the history of CFS and current treatment approaches for both adults and children.

Periodicals

CFIDS Chronicle, "Reduced Blood Volume Targeted," May–June 1998.

Geoffrey Cowley with Mary Hager and Nadine Joseph, "Chronic Fatigue Syndrome: A Modern Medical Mystery," *Newsweek*, November 12, 1990.

Hillary Johnson, "Journey into Fear: The Growing Nightmare of Epstein-Barr Virus," *Rolling Stone*, July 16–30, 1987.

Anthony Whitmars, "The Disappearance of Neurasthenia," *Emerge*, Summer 1998.

Ron Winslow, "CDC to Study Illness Derided As 'Yuppie Flu,'" *Wall Street Journal*, November 19, 1990.

Internet Sources

Michelle Akers, "My History with CFIDS," Soccer Outreach

International. www.socceroutreach.com.

Vicki L. Carpman, "Cognitive Behavioral Therapy: Implications for CFS," *CFIDS Chronicle*. www.cfids.org.

CFIDS Association of America, "Orthostatic Intolerance," www.cfids.org.

CFIDS Chronicle, "Twins Study Looks for Genetic Link." www.cfids.org.

David Futrelle, "Making Ourselves Sick: Are Chronic Fatigue and Gulf War Syndromes Real Physical Illnesses, or Are They All in Our Heads?" *Salon*, August 1997. www.salon.com.

Mark Giuliucci, "Study: Most Lyndonville Children Report At Least Mild Improvement," *CFIDS Chronicle*. www.cfids.org.

Ian Smith, "Drug Could Help Chronic Fatigue: Syndrome Linked to Red Blood Cell Production," WNBC, May 15, 2002. www.wnbc.com.

Television and Radio Sources

Amy Peterson, interview by Jamie Gangel, Today NBC, February 8, 2002.

Index

Rowe, Peter, 73
Royal Free Hospital, 15–17
school phobia, 30, 32–33
Seabiscuit: An American Legend
   (Hillenbrand), 68
separation anxiety disorder, 30
Sharpe, Michael, 75
skin conditions, 38
skull, pressure at base of, 26
sleep, 40
sleep hygiene, 61
Sterling, Jon, 44
Stewart, Julian, 73
stress, 52, 64

teenagers, 44
Teitelbaum, Jacob, 49–50, 63
tender spots, 40
testosterone, 52
thyroid, 52
Today Show (television show), 70
tricyclics, 58
triggers, 54–55

twins, 71–72
Umbro, 69
University of Miami, 74
University of Washington, 71
urination, 38

Verrillo, Erica F., 24, 33, 35, 51,
   53, 64
viral load, 59
viruses, 46–49
vision problems, 38
vitamin supplements, 59–60

Wall Street Journal
   (newspaper), 21
water quality, 54
Winslow, Ron, 21
women, 23, 38, 50

yeast, 49
Yuppie Flu, 20
yuppies, 17–19

Picture Credits

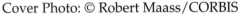

About the Author

Liesa Abrams has written and edited many books for young readers on a diverse range of topics. She is also a regular contributor to a website providing articles on different health issues for children, teens, and parents. She lives in the New York metropolitan area with her husband, Sean.